Personal Logbook

Matthew and Terces Engelhart

Dedicated to our children:
Matthew, Mollie, Molly,
Ryland and Cary

North Atlantic Books
Berkeley, California

Published by
North Atlantic Books   Cover art by Frank Riccio
P.O. Box 12327   Cover and book design by Julia D. Stege
Berkeley, California 94712   Production by Dan Yokum

Printed in Hong Kong by Norcal Printing, San Francisco

First published by With the Current, 2005, San Francisco, California.

The Abounding River Personal Logbook: An Unfamiliar View of Being Abundance is sponsored by the Society for the Study of Native Arts and Sciences, a nonprofit educational corporation whose goals are to develop an educational and crosscultural perspective linking various scientific, social, and artistic fields; to nurture a holistic view of arts, sciences, humanities, and healing; and to publish and distribute literature on the relationship of mind, body, and nature.

North Atlantic Books' publications are available through most bookstores. For further information, call 800-337-2665 or visit our website at www.northatlanticbooks.com.

Substantial discounts on bulk quantities are available to corporations, professional associations, and other organizations. For details and discount information, contact our special sales department.

Library of Congress Cataloging-in-Publication Data

Engelhart, Matthew.
    The abounding river personal logbook : an unfamiliar view of being abundance / by Matthew and Terces Engelhart.
        p. cm.
    Summary: "Presents the authors's practice of being abundance and invites the reader to practice being someone who loves one's life, adores oneself, accepts the world, is generous and grateful everyday, and experiences being provided for"—Provided by publisher.
    ISBN-13: 978-1-55643-709-0
    ISBN-10: 1-55643-709-9
    1. Life. 2. Spirituality. I. Engelhart, Terces, 1950- II. Title.
    BD431.E27 2007
    170'.44—dc22
                                2007022808

1 2 3 4 5 6 7 8 9 Norcal 14 13 12 11 10 09 08 07

Introduction to the Abounding River

Hi,

this is Terces
and
this is Matthew
and we welcome you to The
Abounding River. The
main text of the book is
printed in black,
Terces' personal stories are
in red
and
Matthew's are printed in
blue.

"We worship what
we give our
attention to…"

This is our way of writing the book together and giving
you the opportunity to see what we point out from vary-
ing perspectives. What we offer is simple, age old and
what we call "unfamiliar", or not the common agreed
upon way of viewing what it is to BE ABUNDANCE.

We will ask questions, share with you and ask you to share,
inviting you to look and discover for yourself what it is to
live a plentiful life, no matter what your circumstances may
be, and this is an experiment in how "who you are being"
alters the flow of resources into your life.

This is a Spiritual perspective and practice and is designed for
people who already have a Spiritual connection in their lives,
or for those who are willing to open up to one, particularly
in the area of abundance! Which may only look like you are
simply tired of living with LACK!

No matter how you came to pick up this book, that you
picked up this book makes all the difference. This is the
beginning of your ABOUNDING RIVER journey.

We are gladly accompanying you. Thank you for joining us,

Matthew and Terces Engelhart

A Look at the Map

"You have to believe in gods to see them."
Hopi saying

As this Hopi saying suggests we have to believe that God exists to experience God; there is no empiric evidence. Where can we stand to get a glimpse of God? How can we possibly step outside the totality of life and look for evidence of a wholeness? Where would we be standing? This reminds me of a friend who while in a romantic relationship pines over whether her sweetheart is "the one," as if "the one" exists separate from her saying so. Diving in and declaring "the love of your life" requires faith, devotion and surrender but it is the only way we know to see "the love of your life" and be a part of a whole relationship. Does the lover exist separate from the beloved? Is there a God-experience with no devotee? Perhaps the price of admission is our participation.

"Faith begins with an experiment and ends with an experience."
W.R. Inge

We inherited our experience of linear time, aloneness, survival and death. It is etched in our genes since the days of hunting wooly mammoths. "Stay safe and close to the fire," is the agreed upon strategy. This is our obsession. There is a world *out there* to manipulate, defend against, hoard against, survive and conquer. This ancient tale is the water we swim in, it is fused in our being. It is present the moment we awaken. Some version of competition and scarcity is so hard wired within us that it is invisibly shaping our moment-to-moment experience. In our internal dialogue it might register like this:

"Something is wrong with me, something is wrong with them, I'm not enough, they aren't enough, it shouldn't be this way, I made a mistake, what if...? What do they want?"

This sense of scarcity is systemic. In our being it rarely occurs like a choice or a belief we persistently hold fast or assent to consciously. In this book we take the position that our scarcity tale is inherited, practiced and fueled by widespread agreement. The condition of our world we suggest is a result of our collective habit of being alone, unfulfilled, and not enough.

We are declaring anew what so many mapmakers have previously:

"Consider the ravens: for they neither sow nor reap; which neither have storehouse nor barn and God feedeth them: how much more are ye then the fowls?"

Luke 12:23–25

Abundance, living in the assurance of being provided for, is our Divine inheritance and the only proof is in the declaring and living of it. Consider the Dali Lama of Tibet, who creates the Chinese invasion of Tibet as an opportunity and stimulus for his people. Does he speak the truth? The evidence is the experience of living as a part of one whole life. Being Abundance, being that we are provided for requires that we relinquish what we know and what makes sense to us.

This is our experiment to seek first the Kingdom, to declare a world of plenty and then surrender to the assurance of all those things added. This is the essence of what we give our life to and this book is an expression of who we've been called to be.

An Unfamiliar View

> "Let one therefore keep the mind pure, for what a man thinks, that he becomes."
> *The Upanishads*

> "All that we are is a result of what we have thought. The mind is everything. What we think, we become."
> *Buddha*

This book is about our, Matthew and Terces', practice of being Abundance. In the first ninety pages we discuss our experience, our beliefs, and the truth that we choose to empower. Matthew's personal story is written in blue while Terces' is written in red. Our intention is to inspire you to embark on your own adventure. You don't have to agree with us to participate in the 42-day practice, which is laid out in the next eighty-four pages. It is in the living of abundance that one experiences the current of *The Abounding River*.

This book addresses our attention, our consciousness as the source of our experience of fulfillment and of being supplied with the resources that support our physical existence: money, food, shelter, vacations, hot showers, etc. *Our premise is that out of who we are being –what we think, what we say, what we believe, how we act and what attitude we have – we choose our experience. More accurately put, who we are being frames what part and how*

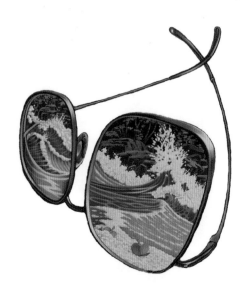

much of life's already perfect magnificence we are present to. This is an age-old perspective.

While variants of this conversation are validated in most scriptures and spiritual paths, the notion that our consciousness is the source of our experience of material wealth is not widely upheld. For example, as of this writing, the media is full of agreement that "we" (the whole world) are in an "economic downturn." as if the conditions described are disconnected from those who are describing them. As human beings it is so easy for us to see the world as something *out there*. We so often live as if life is happening to us; it is something to figure out and master. In this book we take the view that there is no *out there*. We ask you to consider that our experience of life is sculpted by what we're thinking, what we're saying, what we believe, what we're doing and what our attitude is. In this light one begins to understand that to declare an "economic downturn" is to perpetuate it.

In 1984 I was 28, married and had two young children. I was a carpenter by default and my experience was we had no money. I remember wanting to go to the movies one night and scrounging for lost change in the sofa cushions. On my father's 70th birthday, my family missed the celebration. I had neither a car that would make the five-hour trip nor the money to rent one. While I longed for more material security, I rationalized my circumstances as the result of my Spiritual focus. I believed that Spirit and matter were irreconcilable. I "chose" the Spiritual life. I was sure money and God were not compatible. I couldn't see that one aspect of my belief system was a smoke screen for playing it safe and avoiding failure in something I termed the "real world."

Life's current began revealing to me that material abundance and my spiritual values were not exclusive. I joined a group studying "A Course in Miracles" and in a session I declared that I would "make" $10,000 in the month of September, I wrote my promise on a piece of paper. It was April and I had never made even one-fifth that amount in any given month. Soon my declaration was forgotten. In August a commercial roofing job came to my attention. The job was way beyond my skills requiring specialized equipment and training. I bid it without any experience and without a clue of how I would get it done. I received the contract, subcontracted commercial roofers, and profited $10,000 in September. It was a month later I remembered my written declaration and awakened to the connection between my word and my world.

"So shall my word be that goeth forth out of my mouth: it shall not return to me void, but it shall accomplish that which I please, and it shall prosper in the thing whereto I sent it."
Isaiah 55:11

"The currents of
the Universal Being
circulate through me;
I am part and parcel
of God."
Ralph Waldo Emerson

"Most assuredly I
say to you, he who
believes in me, the
works that I do he will
also do; and greater
works than these he
will do."

John 14:12

A year later I began work-ing with a spiritual teacher, Janice Kinney, and she introduced me to a whole new vision. She proposed that matter is Spirit, money is Spirit, I am Spirit, and there is no place Spirit isn't. God is One, indivisible (we are the ones who sub-divide God), One whole body working for and as One Whole All. Quite simply she proposed that our **only** job as human beings is to be aware of and, present to the "Whole" life already is. She said the Whole or God could be known through the qualities of God; Love, Compassion, Abundance, Perfect Health, Joy, Divine Order, etc. These "flavors" of Spirit are our access to the experience of Spirit, of Wholeness. By keeping our attention, our conscious-ness on these qualities of Spirit, we can awaken to the God we are and experience those qualities, including Abundance, the assurance of material supply.

I was immediately con-fronted and exhilarated. With this new view I be-came aware of and grappled with my old patterns of lack and limitation. Was I worthy of being a recipient of heavenly treasure? Could I own myself as a Divine Creation? Was I deserving of an abundant life NOW and ready to be totally responsible for my experi-ence? Was I ready to own my attention, my aware-ness as the source of my supply?

As I started to practice keeping my attention on these qualities of Spirit a struggle ensued. In contrast to being a God worthy of an abundant life now, I noticed my old habits of mind screaming for domi-nation, "This is crazy," "It won't work," "I'm not worthy," "I'm not respon-sible," "Rich people are..." My ego, that part of me that insists on being sepa-rate and feeling threatened, will never accept the Wholeness of Spirit, or Abundance.

As I began to practice I was excited by what I began to see as possible however I also became aware of how old and practiced my "less than" view of myself was.

Even though several years earlier as part of my own journey I had let go of nearly everything I owned and traveled around the country "knowing" we would always be provided for, it still felt scary and uncertain to be that trusting once again.

I had also experienced the freedom of not being attached and knew from experience that "things" come easily when I am open and willing and that hoarding only clogs the flow, and still I experienced caution and mistrust. My identity battled for not letting go again!

Abundance is a condition of wholeness and completeness. Abundance, like God is all-inclusive. Ego will never align with this as it insists on being an outsider.

On the Abounding River we will want to be responsible for our seemingly dual nature, our human habitual self (Ego) and our Spirit Self. Now let's start at the source with the innocence of a child, and together ease into the current of Infinite Supply.

Be willing to be a beginner every single morning..."
Meister Eckhart

"There is only one consciousness, equally distributed everywhere."
Ramana Maharshi

This is a spiritual practice. To take this journey we ask that you begin to consider that life operates as One body, that Spirit is everywhere and is always present! The seen and the unseen universe is all one song. Creation is a cheerleader, a champion for and of it Self and all its parts. This isn't so far fetched.

Fifty years ago the science of Ecology was all but unknown. We were unconscious of the web of life-the interdependence and interplay of the inanimate and animate worlds. We now know a volcano in the South Pacific can impact deer populations in maritime Canada, the weather in Antarctica, sunsets in Seattle and tuna migration patterns worldwide. Scientists now recognize that the earth works as one system.

The honeybee and the apple blossom exist seemingly separate as parts of one whole process. The kidney and the heart are in total alignment for each other as one body. We're proposing that our next step is to recognize that God is its work. That Spirit is One, expressing as many, always expressing as more of it Self. There is an innate benevolence to life, as Spirit loves all of Spirit. This is the nature of Spirit; God is the cause and recipient of everything. Nothing happens that isn't for the whole cosmos and for all the parts.

"The eye with which I see God is the same eye by which God sees me."
Meister Eckhart

"Not an atom moves except by God's will."
Ramana Maharshi

In this book we mostly use the word "Spirit" to represent life as One Unified Field- OneWholeness. We also use Oneness, Wholeness, Source, One, The Divine, God, Self, Eternal Presence. You could use, Energy, Nature, Love, Gaia, Allah, or any name that calls to you.

"It is God Himself who is sporting in the form of man."
Ramakrishna

"Everyman is divinity in disguise, a god playing a fool."
Ralph Waldo Emerson

Spirit is everywhere, always present and that includes you, me, this book, money, and all of life. Spirit is perfect because Spirit is all there is. Consider that we are all perfect; perfect like a newborn babe, as perfect as this moment, as this moment is all there is. We are all Divine masterpieces- Picassos and Rembrandts- playing the charade of "just trying to pay the bills" or pretending to be "works in progress." On this river we are remembering to

embrace ourselves as perfect, as perfect as the sky is blue, as intrinsically beautiful as the Grand Canyon, right now. Being Abundance is thinking, speaking, believing, acting and having an attitude of whole, complete, and fulfilled now. There is nowhere to get. Where would there be to get to? Where could God go? What does God need?

"There is no greater mystery then this, that we keep seeking reality though in fact we are reality. We think that there is something hiding our reality and that this must be destroyed before reality is gained. How ridiculous! A day will dawn when you will laugh at all your past efforts. That which will be on the day you laugh is also here and now."
Ramana Maharshi

Our ego is not going to like going with the current of the Abounding River. By ego I mean that part of us that is separate by nature, alone, and afraid. The part of us that is sure there is always something missing. The ingrate in our head that finds all in the course of one single moment something wrong with others, the world, or ourselves. We propose that ego and scarcity are synonymous. Both are birthed by the illusion of separation. Ego perceives itself as separate, separate from Spirit, separate from the present moment, separate from abundance. Abundance and oneness threaten Ego, whose job it is to exclude, so it is defensive, a hoarder, and a survivalist. Ego believes that death is real, and ego always has somewhere important to get to, something important to do. This morning in yoga the instructor said, "After class you'll be able to tackle the world." Our ego is so convinced life has to be wrestled to the ground.

"Only the threatened attack."
A Course in Miracles

Ego is the source of our human scarcity experience. Some version of being alone, on our own, up against it, is ego's relentless monologue. I don't want you to hear that ego is bad. Rather, ego is merely the *illusion* of separation. It is a paradox. Ego serves a purpose by providing a wonderful contrast that allows us to know aloneness in order that we might appreciate ourselves as part of the whole indivisible Spirit. We are all prodigal sons and daughters returning home. The why of ego or the illusion of separation is not the concern of this book. Nor are we advocating the overthrow of the ego. Our concern is inviting ego to be an observant passenger rather then the insistent driver of our lives.

While the paradigm of scarcity is ancient, inherited and fortified with heaps of evidence, *we say it is simply practiced*. As human beings we have become patrons of "the world is scary," safe and separate is our mold. It is only in the human world where individuality is exalted that scarcity can exist. If we weren't so all consumed with the survival of the "me," we'd have no concern for not enough or getting ahead.

A huge file of evidence for being separate bolsters our habit of scarcity. Listen to your own internal dialogue, the speaking of others, or the media. The over all themes are some version of:

"SOMETHINGS WRONG!" "How can God let this happen?" "There is no God," "I should be...," "I'm lazy," "I'm fat," "I'm messed up," "This shouldn't be," "This should be."

Matthew and I continue practicing keeping our attention on qualities of Spirit (God, Higher Self, etc.) and even though I wiggled and squirmed in the beginning and often felt silly or unattached to what I was saying, we kept our practice up. A few times we would miss a couple of days and both of us noticed that the old fears of lack and scarcity would come creeping back into our awareness. We often share with people in our workshops that we (you and I) are always keeping our attention on something so why not keep it on being qualities of Spirit? If we don't create something we will fall back on some version of our default thinking of something's wrong or something's missing.

What version of "something's wrong" are you listening to?

We call this a *recurrent*, ego's whirlpool that keeps us out of the flow of life and battered by the illusion of scarcity. The recurrent we entertain or indulge in frequently frames our view of life. When caught in a recurrent there is no ease, peace or fulfillment; suffering and longing are present. Here are some signals, some alarms that indicate our ego is in control and we are caught in a recurrent.

" We experience opposites; them, and us, sides, or positions.
" We are using "should" or "have to."
" Life is black or white, either, or.
" We are blaming or justifying
" Our attention is in the future-Fear or expectation is present.
" Our attention in the past-guilt or regret is present.
" There is somewhere to get to. It is better over there than here.
" We are being significant-life is serious.
" Something is MISSING now.
" Something is WRONG now!

In this way ego keeps us on a short leash. Fearing the annihilation of the present moment, ego will always throw a wrench in the works with some version of something's wrong. A recurrent is always some version of *something's wrong*. Just listen to your own internal dialogue for a while and notice all the variants of "something's wrong" that pass through your consciousness.

Terces and I often ask each other, "What version of 'something's wrong,' are you listening to?" If I look there is almost always something undone that I'm punishing myself for, a bill to pay, a request I haven't responded to, a call to make, someone I'm judging or some place other then here and now to get to. My predominate recurrent is "I should be_____." I can fill in the blank with almost anything.

A less obvious and more pervasive version of resisting, the all-providing flow of life, is our addiction to *knowing*. We are steeped in inherited and deeply imbedded myths about *how life is*. There are ways we simply *know* life is that are so in the background of our awareness we rarely notice or examine them and yet they are the filters through which Spirit-all of life- is received, perceived and experienced. These beliefs and cultural attitudes are passed down, accepted and woven into the narrative of our life. We encourage you to challenge your beliefs, dig underneath them and see where they came from and what is really keeping them in place. You may discover you have all kinds of contradicting beliefs or attitudes when it comes to money and supply.

Here are a few examples of myths that might go unquestioned:

- There is never enough
- Life is a struggle
- You can never get ahead, it's always going to be this way
- Money is the root of all evil
- Failure is bad
- When things are going well something bad always happens
- It is better to give than receive
- There's a "real" world separate from a "spiritual" world
- More is better
- Someday I'll be happy
- Death is bad
- People can't be trusted

What we don't realize is that we are practicing these myths and they are keeping us apart from the whole of life; they steep us in scarcity, and they have become our tales. Tall tales we tell one another and ourselves over and over again. Our egos cling to them because ego has zero tolerance for not knowing. We are all master storytellers of our own particular version of "the truth." Unbeknownst to ourselves we are the ones who propagate and uphold **how life is** for fear of surrendering to the abounding current of the unknown and innocence.

This reaction to "unexplored territory" can be expressed as an acronym as a way of reminding ourselves of the grip the paradigm of scarcity has on our lives:

P.A.S.T.,
Practiced, Apart, Scarcity, Tale.

"We empty ourselves to be filled with God. Even God cannot fill what is full."
Mother Theresa

The illustration depicting the P.A.S.T. (See page 15) is a backwater of stagnation out of the current of life because ego's conviction is that life's never going to be any different and ego has a heap of evidence."

*"My grand daddy told me **never** to borrow money from a friend."*

Resignation and cynicism are the cost of this unquestioned narrative. Ego keeps us safe and close to the fire with its storytelling.

I have a saying, "Safe is a sedative." The comfort zone of what we "know" is a cage of tedious malaise. By the warmth of the fire we are surviving life rather than graciously receiving what the river has in store for us just around the next bend.

Spotting a recurrent or a piece of our P.A.S.T is an opportunity to practice something new, to hand-pick a sun ripened thought, to create anew what you say, your beliefs, your actions, and your attitudes. To be or choose to put your attention on a quality of Spirit -joy, happiness,

love, abundance, etc. The persistence of our ego is extraordinary.

The other day a friend asked to borrow some money. I declined and was immediately thrashing in a recurrent, "I'm selfish," "I used be about making a difference," "I'm not generous..." I experienced guilt. If I had said, "yes," to the request, my internal dialogue would have run something like this: "What about _my_ commitments?   I sold out again. I can never say no. Mr. Nice Guy strikes again." My ego's only investment in either response was keeping me separate.

Ego is only interested in surviving-remaining in control. Ego is the Michael Jordan of judgment, assessment, and evaluation. Something is always wrong or missing, with me, with you, with the world. Egos only interest is keeping us up against the ropes, just out of arm's reach of being fulfilled in the present moment.

As I sit here right now writing, I am in our studio in Hawaii on our 13-acre farm on the island of Maui. It is absolutely beautiful here. The farm is lush and full of papayas, mangoes, bananas, avocados, coffee, lilikoi and other exotic fruits. We just finished preparing a delicious lunch all from farm-grown produce and we ate it in an amazing outdoor kitchen.

We were walking back to the studio when I realized that I hadn't noticed the fresh pineapple sitting on the counter that had been given to us when we arrived, so I asked Matthew, "Did you see the pineapple in the kitchen?" He was walking just ahead of me and called back. "No." IMMEDIATELY in my head a conversation started up, "See you shouldn't have taken it into the kitchen, now someone else has eaten it." "You should have eaten it this morning and not have saved it for later." ON AND ON THIS CONVERSATION WENT! "That was the first pineapple you were going to have from the farm." " There aren't that many pineapples yet."

When I tried to remind myself that it was just a pineapple and everything was still great the conversation went off in another direction. "See how selfish you really are, the only person you really care about is you." "Notice it didn't seem to bother Matthew that it wasn't there, why can't you be more like him!" It didn't seem to matter what direction I went there was always some come back, some quick answer that still had me experiencing being separate, coming from scarcity, something being wrong.

Only when I shared with Matthew what I was experiencing and we laughed at the insidiousness of a recurrent did I begin to feel an easing of the tension that was permeating my entire body.

A little after 5 o'clock we walked back up to our outdoor kitchen to prepare fresh juice "cocktails" and as we stepped through the doorway we looked up and there was the pineapple sitting on the counter! We looked at one another and started laughing!

This is such a great example of a RECURRENT. Notice there was no truth to any of my thoughts... the pineapple hadn't been eaten, it hadn't even moved! Notice ego didn't care, it will go off in any direction without any requirement for what is really so. The next morning we ate the pineapple for breakfast and it was delicious!

"Wisdom is not found in making divisions and comparisons."
Maitreya

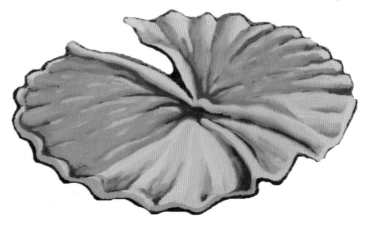

"One of ego's favorite paths of resistance is to fill you with doubt."

Ram Dass

I am reminded of Charlie Chaplin's angst on his way to the opening debut of "City Lights." At the time, 1931, he was perhaps the most successful artist on the planet and one of the most popular and adored people as well. He was completely terrified that his still silent "little tramp" would not be accepted in the new age of talkies. Even with all his talent (he wrote, directed, acted in and wrote the musical scores for his films), track record, fame, wealth and beautiful women his ego had him in a state of panic, not trusting himself, his life and audience. "City Lights" appears on many film critics' top ten all time film lists. It is a heartfelt classic.

Ego is insatiable. I went to Hawaii for the first time in 1987. I was thrilled to stay in a rat infested shack and trade rent for carpentry. The idea of owning property there was unimaginable. By 1995 we bought a 13-acre farm a few minutes walk from a beach. A few years later I wanted ocean front property. Ego is never satisfied. Being fulfilled occurs like death to the ego. Ego is the taskmaster, fixing, solving, strategizing all to avoid being complete and present here and now.

Terces' Mom has been told she has less than a year to live. She owns her home, she has plenty of medical insurance and money. Still she fills her day finding the best price on cantaloupe or figuring out whether she

can claim a broken window on her home without increasing her insurance premium.

When I first started exploring the being of abundance I was sharing the possibility with my bookkeeper, probably evangelically. She said to me, "Matthew, I don't want to make money a priority in my life." I said to her, "Jeannie, how often do you think about buying your son a new bike, sending your parents on a cruise or owning your own house?" She said, "Oh, all the time." I said, "It already is a priority, maybe even an all consuming one, perhaps there is a whole new way to think about money that would give you some freedom."

Look at your life. How much of your attention is consumed by strategy about money, survival or getting somewhere? How much of your awareness is occupied by giving thanks for all you have received?

Sometimes our persistent concern about money looks like avoidance as seen in the following example.

We gave our first Abounding River workshop to our community in Hawaii. In a conversation about dealing with money my nephew

Josh shared that he tried to manage his money by paring his life down to three bills- propane, car insurance, and telephone. To my friend Buck, a retired and very successful entrepreneur, dealing with money is so upsetting that he uses a bill paying service so he has to write only one check a month. Neither claimed that their strategies relieved them from their gnawing concern about money.

What is your existing relationship with money and supply?

My family upbringing was focused on being kind and giving to others while being practical and thrifty when it came to money. Everything had a cost and

there was always a conversation about whether or not it was worth it? We were taught to save money and take care of whatever we had so it would last longer, if not forever. We had "good" dishes and silverware that were reserved for times when we had company. We rarely ate in restaurants for my Mother could make a better meal for less at home. My experience of abundance is summed up in a childhood memory of, living in Cuba as a youngster. My sisters and I would ride our horses to the Officers Club, pay for an iced tea, then take the lemon wedge and squeeze it into a paper cup at the water fountain, add sugar and that way get two drinks for the price of one! The rest of my life is pretty much some version of this scenario or a reaction to it. I have worked hard and long hours as a single mother with three children and been thrifty and creative in meeting our needs. Our support and love for each other is most important and we've always experienced having just enough. Most of my life I have owned my own business.

One of the first things we discovered in our workshop is that people don't openly talk about their relationship with money, in some cases it is taboo. People are more likely to talk about the last time they had sex rather than their net worth! Most people don't even think about their relationship to money as a relationship, what if you did?

Consider that money is your friend whom you have had a relationship with for a long time, perhaps since your first lemonade stand or allowance.

We are going to do an exercise here and the money (your friend) is going to ask you several questions. Simply listen for what the money asks and write down your answer without editing your response.

Money is asking you these questions.
1. Is our relationship security for you?
2. Do you expect me to make you happy?
3. Are you afraid of me?
4. Are you proud of our relationship?
5. Do you love me?
6. Do you tell the truth about our relationship? (Are you open to speak about our relationship freely?)
7. Is there anything else you would like to say to me?

Can you see that if you treated your loved ones like you treat your relationship to money they probably wouldn't stay around? This exercise may give you some insights into why your relationship with money looks the way it does. You may even be surprised by some of your answers.

What are some of your inherited beliefs about money?

Money doesn't grow on trees is one of mine, along with it's better to give than to receive and the harder I work the luckier I get, I remember needle pointing that one and hanging it on my wall for years.

Money isn't important is one of mine, another version of that is, if you put too much attention on money you've sold out on what matters.

Here are some beliefs that others have shared with us. Notice we often contradict ourselves when it comes to our beliefs about money.

¨ I have to work hard to make money.
¨ You can't make money doing what you love.
¨ It is wrong to receive assistance from others; you should support yourself.
¨ It's all about whom you know.
¨ I should help people who are in need.
¨ People I give money to probably misuse it.
¨ No one should make that much money.
¨ If I don't have enough money something bad will happen.
¨ People without money are unhappy, don't have anything to offer.
¨ People without money live simpler lives and have fewer worries.
¨ There is never enough money.
¨ Once I get money it's hard to keep it.
¨ I can't accomplish my dreams without money
¨ It takes money to make money
¨ Money is power.
¨ Money can't make me happy
¨ I can't be happy without money.
¨ I should save money.
¨ You should make your own money.
¨ Money is private.

This inherited scarcity tale, ego's program, is systemic and entrenched. It is a "view of life" that has life looking like a flood of circumstances against which we must swim.

We are saying that abundance is another possible view of life. It is a context from which to live or a way of being alive that gives one access to the Divine.

In the Christian tradition, charitable is a way of being that gives one access to Spirit or Oneness. In Sufism being or practicing ecstatic love is another.

In Buddhism compassion is yet another doorway. We are saying that being abundance is a way of being alive, a way to worship, a practice in awakening to what already is.

What is Abundance?

"We walk by faith not by sight."

Corrinthians 5:7

"If God so clothe the grass, which is today in the field, and to-morrow is cast into the oven: how much more will he clothe you, O Ye of little faith."

Luke 12:28

"Only the loving find love, They never have to seek for it."

D.H. Lawrence

We are saying that abundance is a quality of Spirit, one of the flavors of the Divine along with joy, happiness, love, freedom, health, creativity, etc. These are our divine birthright; in fact, we are saying these qualities are always present, even though we aren't always present to them. By abundance we mean "the assurance and knowingness of being supplied." By supply we mean the resources that support our material existence, for example; money, food, shelter, clothing, vacations, hot water, street cleaning, parks, music, tools, gasoline, transportation, etc. Notice it may be easier to think of joy, love or happiness as spiritual attributes and it may be a bit of a stretch to think of abundance particularly an abundance of supply as a property of the Divine.

This book is about *being abundance*, living in the assurance of being supplied as a mindful practice to connect to Spirit in everything. In being peaceful we have peace, in being loving our experience is love, or in being joyful we are present to joy. These qualities don't exist *out there*.

We are saying being abundance is our access to experiencing abundance – the assurance and knowingness of being supplied. Abundance is a quality of Spirit, meaning it is always present, just like love or joy, etc. We are present to abundance by being assured.

The stock market and the economy are a vivid demonstration of this principle. The "value" of the nation's businesses is beholden to our moment-by-moment consumer and investor confidence. The worth of a company may vary greatly in one day because of its perceived value regardless of its "real" assets.

Our collective experience of financial well-being is based on our ability to trust in our financial well-being. Trust and confidence are not bound by outer conditions- they're always available.

Look and see if your own prosperity barometer, your experience of economic fulfillment is a function of the faith, confidence and trust you have in yourself and your life. Regardless of our circumstances, our balance sheet, our indebtedness, we propose that our moment-to-moment awareness of material well-being is a function of conviction.

"Let us learn to think of dollars as we do leaves on trees, or oranges, as the natural and inevitable result of the law active within. There is truly no need to worry even when the trees appear to be bare, as long as we are conscious of the truth that the law is even now operating within to bring forth fruit after it's own kind. Regardless of the state of our finances, at any given moment, let us not be concerned or worried because we know that the law acting in, through, and as our consciousness is at work within us, when we are asleep as well as when we are awake, to provide all those added things."

Joel Goldsmith

What is Being?

"The tree which moves some to tears of joy is in the eyes of others a green thing which stands in the way. As a man is so he sees."

William Blake

In this adventure "being" is what we are thinking, what we are saying to others and ourselves, what we believe, how we act, and what our attitude is. Our life experience is who we are being about the circumstances of our life. What we are thinking, speaking, believing, acting or what we attitude about our life is our experience-is our life.

So that this is clear for you let's take a moment and go through each one of these together.

First there is *THOUGHT*, this is what you think about something/someone i.e.: I think I am poor, shy, etc.

Then there is what you *SAY* i.e.: I tell people I can't afford something, I say I am busy when I am not so I can get out of going someplace (because I am shy).

Next there is what you *BELIEVE* i.e.: I believe it is bad to be poor, I believe shyness is something you are born with and I will always be this way. Are you clear what a belief is? It is something that you believe is true for you; it may even be the source of some of your thoughts. Your beliefs may be inherited or you may have come to believe them. We might say they are at your core, informing your thoughts and actions.

Then there are the *ACTIONS* you take i.e.: I buy only the least expensive items (not even what I want sometimes), I don't go to events with large groups...

And lastly there is the *ATTITUDE* you have: I attitude shame (of being poor), I attitude fearful (of others). This one isn't so obvious. An attitude is unspoken, yet can be expressed in your tone of voice, body language, etc. Most of us have had experiences where we said one thing, but what got communicated was quite different; the difference in the communication was probably our attitude. You could think of this as the flavor of what we are saying or doing.

Can you see how each is distinct and how they all create your experience of life?

"One's own thought is one's world. What a person thinks is what he becomes– That is the eternal mystery."
The Upanishads

When I was forty, I stood on the rim of the Grand Canyon for the first time in my life. All the years of anticipation had not prepared me for the magnitude of my experience. I was awed by the beauty and present to joy. About 20 feet away stood a man with a large trucker's belt buckle on and a baseball cap. I overheard him say to his wife; "You could dump garbage in there for 1000 years and still not fill it." He was having his Grand Canyon experience.

Life is vast and mysterious, and our experience of life is "framed" by our thoughts, speech, beliefs, actions and attitudes.

Notice on any day or at any given moment our experience of our day can swing dramatically from peaceful to agitated, from fulfilled to unappreciated, and from inspired to re-signed. The circumstances are often the same, but who we are being about those circumstances shifts our experience. Again, being is what we are think-ing, speaking, believing, acting and our attitude about our life.

Have you ever been on vacation, surrounded by ideal circumstances and been miserable? Have you ever been unable to appreciate a beautiful sunset or enjoy your own children because of the clamor in your head? Have you ever been washing the dishes or scrubbing the floor and been happy and fulfilled?

As human beings we are always trying to manage the circumstances of our life. When all the while it is who we are being about our life that gives us our life experience. Our educational system is geared toward doing, having, getting somewhere and it is devoid of any training in being.

The scarcity paradigm is all about having the **right** circumstances and then being happy, fulfilled, etc. Our inherited view of life is **get** this and then **be** that. Advertising fortifies the **get this then be that** matrix.

Ask almost anyone how their day was and they will likely tell you about something that happened or some circumstance as the reason they are happy, disappointed, hopeful, etc.

We can be grateful to countless human beings who have demonstrated that life arises out of who one is being- that being outshines what we have or what happened. Nelson Mandela, the gracious political prisoner of Apartheid, Ernest Shackelton, the enduring and courageous Antarctic explorer, and Mahatma Gandhi, India's beloved humanitarian activist are three extreme examples of how the power of being is victorious over circumstances and conditions. Elvis Presley, Judy Garland and Howard Hughes are three examples of how exalted circumstances (wealth, talent, success) guarantee nothing.

"We don't see things as they are, we see them as we are."
Anais Nin

"If a pickpocket meets a Saint he only sees pockets."
Baba Hari Das

"It's not the size of the dog in the fight, it's the size of the fight in the dog."

Kit Raymond

I have extraordinary circumstances in my life. I live with an incredible woman; Terces who completely adores me, I can't imagine someone loving me more nor can I imagine loving another more. We live in my favorite neighborhood in San Francisco, and have a phenomenal view of the city. We own a 13-acre organic farm in Maui minutes from a private beach. We have 5 healthy children that we adore and that adore us. We have plenty of money. We meditate and practice Pranayama (yogic breathing) and hatha yoga everyday. We eat the best organic live natural food. Our health is vibrant. We have friends around the world that love us and our community empowers us as leaders. Our service of training people in the being of abundance is rewarding and fulfilling work. We recently took a month to cross the country in our VW camper visiting family and friends. I love my life!

Do these conditions guarantee my happiness or satisfaction? Being fulfilled is a moment-by-moment choice. By default I will engage and empower some programmed long standing version of," I'm not enough," or " I should be doing more." Before I know it I will be worrying that my life is going to fall apart and I will be left alone in the gutter and people will be talking about me saying, " He used to be the Abundance Guy."

When I'm caught in that swirl my beautiful wife and my outstanding view of the San Francisco Bay all but disappear.

When I was sixteen I was a competitive swimmer, I had been working out since I was a young child. I was very strong and in excellent physical condition and competed on a national level; however I thought I was fat.

My internal voice was always judging me and comparing me to others, when I looked in the mirror it was to see how fat I looked. In the following year I tried to lose weight and couldn't so I stopped eating, eventually I developed an eating disorder and continued to lose weight. No matter how much weight I lost, even when I weighed only ninety pounds; I still looked fat to me! Over the next twenty years my physical appearance (or circumstances) had nothing to do with what I saw in the mirror; what I thought, what I was saying (especially to myself), what I believed were all calling the shots.

My experience of myself had nothing to do with what you and I call reality, it was only who I was being that was creating my experience. I've looked back at pictures of myself and thought, "What was I thinking?"

Perhaps we all have some sort of distorted picture of our lives and ourselves; and it is just invisible to us. We spend all our energy trying to change the outer picture when really what there is to attend to is the inner being.

What circumstances in your life have you been or are you trying to change? Now take a look at what YOU are thinking, speaking, believing, acting and what your attitude is that is creating your experience of those circumstances.

Life is life and what we are thinking, speaking, believing, acting and what attitude we have about life is *our life*- our experience. Why do we mostly have life so backwards? Why do we put so much emphasis on the doing, on the managing of the outer circumstances, on the getting somewhere, and so little on who we are *being*?

This "backward" approach to life is the source of our scarcity experience. It is like looking at yourself in the mirror and trying to change the image you see by painting on the glass. No matter how much paint you apply to the mirror, there you are. Notice how we fill up our day doing something or getting something accomplished so we can *be* satisfied, as if we are making a deal with ourselves. If I do this *then* I can be _____. Why not start practicing being satisfied and fulfilled *now*?

Notice how we try to escape our internal dialogue by unconsciously over working, taking drugs, shopping till we drop, boob tubing, video gaming, over

eating, etc. How many of us would rather listen to commercial radio than to our own internal monologue? That is an indication of just how yucky the internal conversation can be. Rarely do we practice with much rigor who we are being.

One morning at 5:30 am, on the way to yoga, Terces and I passed a movie theater swarmed with hundreds of people waiting in line for tickets to the newest release of "The Matrix." People will get up early to be entertained; ego wants to be "done" to. There were only six people in yoga class.

Ego is obsessed with the outer experience. Mastery is being the master of our experience, or at the source of it.

We have only to attend to five aspects of being: our thoughts, our speech, our beliefs, our actions and our attitudes. What a celebration! These are our access to everything we want- everything we already are.

We don't often look at life this way but we can hand-pick what thoughts we have, what we say, what we believe, the actions we take and our attitudes.

They may seem automatic and they are (try not thinking or staying completely still for a long time) but those that we frequent, those that impact our lives are the ones we've practiced to the point of becoming habitual. We are indulging in them, we are attending to them and yet it occurs as if we just *are* that way; "I don't make enough money," "I'm not a party person," "I'm not motivated," "I'm too fat," "I'm unorganized," etc. They're practiced and we have mastered that way of being.

This book is about practicing, mastering the *being of abundance*. We call this *Spiritizing*, i.e. attending to the thoughts, speech, beliefs, actions and attitudes that exalt life, choosing to be qualities of Spirit- practicing Oneness.

"We are what we repeatedly do.

Excellence then, is not an act but a habit."
Aristotle

Let's review what we've said so far:

" Spirit is everywhere and is always present. There is nothing that is not Spirit.

" An access to experiencing Spirit is who we are being or being qualities of Spirit.

" Abundance is a quality of Spirit.

" Abundance is always present.

" Our access to Abundance is who we are being.

" Being is what we think, what we say (to ourselves as well as others), what we believe, the actions we take and the attitudes we have.

" We can choose who we are being- our thoughts, speech, beliefs, actions and attitudes.

"A man is what he thinks about all day long."
Ralph Waldo Emerson

Six Ways to Worship

"There are hundreds of ways to kneel and kiss the ground."

Rumi

We have distinguished what we call six **Spirit currents**, six ways of being, six ways to worship, that we say evoke abundance, that bring to one's awareness how plentiful life already is. These six currents keep one in the flow of abundance and present to life and one's self as One complete whole.

This current is the premise that our life is a picture of our thoughts, speech, beliefs, actions and attitudes. Our life experience is sourced by whom we are being. These are the seeds we sow and reap. Spirit in all its' benevolence will empower or illuminate however we are being. If we are being lack Spirit will illuminate an abundance of lack. If we are *wanting* to be rich, Spirit will illuminate wanting, we will have an abundance of wanting. **Spirit is and only expresses as abundance** and we've been given the honor and privilege to determine what form that abundance will take in our lives. So look and see what you experience an abundance of and you will begin to see where you "invest" your attention.

I was a father of two young children in my early twenties. For jobs I cleaned houses, dug graves, picked apples, pruned apple trees, did carpentry, painted houses, I invested my attention in "just enough." I espoused that God always provided just in time and just enough. I always had plenty of "just enough" or "getting by."

In the latter years of my first marriage I had stopped being that my first wife, Jeanne, was the one; I stopped choosing her just the way she was. I wanted her to be different and I received an abundantly different Jeanne- she fell in love with someone else.

"The game of life is the game of boomerangs. Our thoughts, deeds, and words return to us sooner or later with astounding accuracy."

Florence Shinn

"The altering eye alters all."

William Blake

"Be ye transformed by the renewing of your mind."

Romans 12:2

Being responsible is owning that we are the creator of our experience, and then attending to our attention, investing our consciousness in qualities of being we want to experience. Being abundance is thinking, speaking, believing, acting and attituding (I know this is a made up verb) that we are a part of *one whole abundant life* now.

The tricky thing about this is when we start to look outside ourselves to see if we are "having" more or if "it" (this practice)is working, we are not being Spirit.

Spirit can only be whole and complete. If we are being something's missing, if we are looking to see if *more* is there, Spirit will illuminate an abundance of something is missing, or not *more.*

This is a reminder, a gentle nudge to be whole and complete- to adjust our attention, to recognize our Self. The minute we are looking for *more,* we are being *not more,* we are being something's missing.

This is easier to see in the context of a relationship. If instead of being loving we are looking for love in a relationship to show up

over there with our partner, (i.e. "Am I getting what I want?" "Is he or she the one?", "Is this relationship working?"), what we'll experience is a lot of waiting for love to show up- a lot of "not love." We are not being love or experiencing love. Love is a way of being alive that has life be a loving experience. Love is connecting to our Self in others.

We have all met people who demonstrate this or have had glimpses of this ourselves. Mother Theresa comes to mind as someone who presences love, or is responsible for being love in the face of horrendous circumstances- not much could dampen her expressing love.

Abundance is the same. If we are being abundance, living the certainty of being supplied now, if we are gratefully and consciously receiving what

has already been given, we will experience an abundance of supply flowing into our lives. If we withhold supply i.e., pay bills late or just in time, be stingy, or in any way restrict the flow in our part of the *One* body, our experience will be the universe is withholding. In this way we can understand and taste what we are creating-*withholding*.

Abundance means to trust and celebrate the flow in and out of our life but not in order to get more. Remember we can't be looking for *it* because in the looking we are being *not it*.

This is what we think Christ means in the twelfth chapter of Luke when he says, "*Seek ye first the kingdom of Heaven and all else will be given unto you.*"

The paradox of this practice is that we will experience more abundance and forms of supply in our lives but the more we look for evidence, the more we "be" that there is

somewhere to get, that something is missing, that it must look a particular way, we diminish our experience of the flow.

Lots of people come to the Abounding River because they want more, Matthew started his practice years ago because he wanted more, and I wanted him to teach me because I wanted my children to have more.

This isn't however another plan, or strategy to acquire or manifest anything, it is about shifting our awareness to all we already have.

This is a place our egos frequently get in the way, as we have shared the ego has no interest in one being fulfilled and satisfied, so it is constantly pointing out what is missing.

I remember sitting in our beautiful home in San Francisco looking out our office window at the Bay Bridge and experiencing my peace of mind and appreciation being interrupted by thoughts about how long it is taking us to get a small leak in the kitchen ceiling repaired and making myself wrong for it! Can you see the insidiousness of it all?

This practice is the faith experiment in managing oneself as "being plentiful" now and receiving what appears as plentiful now. We are in heaven; the rest is gravy.

"When you realize nothing is lacking, the whole world belongs to you."

Lao Tzu

"All the way to heaven is heaven."

Saint Catherine of Siena

"Doubts arise in the absence of surrender."

Ramana Maharshi

When I was age 30 and discovered the possibility of being abundance. I took on the being of millionaire prior to any evidence or appearances that would validate millionaire. The first thing I had to do was make peace with being rich. As a citizen of the U.S.A, I was already in the first class cabin and I gave up my inherited conversation about rich being bad, not spiritual, etc. I put "post it notes" all over my house with "I am a millionaire," "I am rich," "I love money and money loves me," written on them. I relished our $400 Saab as if it were a Mercedes. I was being that I had access to Divine wealth. I was being first the inward expression of millionaire and the outward expression (in 4-6 years) showed up.

Having most of my life created and worked in my own businesses, I would start out really trusting the creative process, listening to and implementing my internal guidance. Yet when I was confronted or having to deal with some sticky financial situation I would question if my guidance was working, and always feelings of insecurity would arise. Now I can see how I was the one creating the insecurity by putting my attention on doubting.

My life is an experiment, a demonstration that life really is lived from inside out. I still doubt, I look to the outer for the evidence, and sometimes I expect the goodies. When I do Spirit illuminates an abundance of "what's missing" - lack of faith, no fulfillment, an abundance of scarcity. This practice builds muscle in being abundance now. There is nowhere to get, nothing to prove. Fulfillment is a moment-to-moment choice.

We pick our thoughts, our speech, our beliefs, our actions and our attitudes. They create our experience by framing what part of Spirit we are going to be present to. One of the paradoxes of being that we are the creator of our experience is that when we are suffering, struggling, complaining, worrying etc., we are also the creator of THAT experience! Be patient. That isn't going to disappear, there is simply to notice where our attention is and then shift our attention to what we are committed to creating.

Why not create something that is nourishing, inspiring and fulfilling? WHY WOULD WE PICK ANYTHING OTHER THAN WHAT WE WANT FOR OTHERS AND OURSELVES?

Steering our attention from ego's scarcity tale to Spirit's opulence is simply a matter of practice.

I'm still amazed sometimes at the hold my versions of limitation attempt to have on my experience. I live a blessed and magical life and all the old stories of fear, lack, and inadequacy are only a thought away at any moment. All there is for me to manage is keeping my attention on the wonder and bounty of my life NOW.

Every time I get a parking ticket I have a choice, the same eternal choice, presence Spirit or presence scarcity. Am I going to *Spiritize* this moment? I can celebrate the city, be grateful for the clean streets, the parks, garbage

pick-up, homeless shelters, etc. I can relish participating in the salary of a city employee, who is *SpiritMe* over there. I am equally free to indulge in my Ego's scarcity tale. I can choose to get angry with myself, make the city wrong, bolster my experience of separation and go comatose to all that I have in this present moment.

Take a moment and look at your life, what are you creating, remembering you are the creator of your experience of ALL OF IT? Our thoughts are more malleable than we might think, you can create something new, there is simply to practice.

Worth

Worth just might be the toughest current to be in. For example let us consider for just a moment that we are perfect! Just as perfect as everything else Spirit is- the ocean, the sky, a vineyard, a newborn babe.

Now consider we are all whole and complete, there is nowhere to go, there is nothing to prove. Our value is established as a Divine creation. We are perfect! All that is asked of us is to recognize our true Selves.

Are you experiencing this as a HUGE relief? Say to your self out loud, " I am perfect just the way I am; I love me." What is your

internal dialogue saying now? Can you hear a litany of thoughts, perhaps some core beliefs, and encompassing attitudes contrary to your own perfection?

This is what we mean by a tough current to be in. Isn't it just slightly arrogant to argue with the artist? Can you hear your practiced resistance to owning your source and honoring your creator by loving yourself?

When I met Matthew I was closing up my business in Sonoma County, I had begun working for a human awareness organization in a primary leadership role which required long hours, Although I was sleeping on the couch of my two elder children's apartment in the Mission district of San Francisco, and most of my personal belongings were in storage, I was grateful and content.

As confronting as my circumstances were at times I embraced every challenge as an opportunity.

Six months later I went on my first vacation as an adult, with Matthew to Hawaii. Although I had swum in the Bay for years (twice out and around Alcatraz, from the Bay Bridge to the Golden Gate) I had never swum in warm water! Suddenly now I found myself face to face with being worthy of all this grandeur. It wasn't easy for me to take time off, so much of my worth was tied up in being a hard working, high producing individual. Matthew and I would dive into the cresting waves on a private beach; float on our backs looking up at the peaks of Haleakala, and he would say to me, "Isn't it beautiful?" It was a struggle for me to be with so much beauty, I had to surrender to being worthy.

Can you surrender to how beautiful you are?

Our life is an expression of who we are being. If we are thinking, speaking, believing or having an attitude that there is something wrong with us, that we are stupid, lazy, ugly, unorganized, inadequate, etc, our lives will reflect just that- we will have an abundance of feeling stupid, lazy, ugly, unorganized, inadequate, etc.

My friend Jim was struggling financially because a construction project he was responsible for was far exceeding his bid. He was emotionally upset and soon began to feel physically sick. I spoke with him often about declaring bankruptcy and he would reply that he just couldn't do that. For him bankruptcy was the ultimate failure.

Over the next several months he continued to suffer as his financial situation worsened. He whittled his life down to the mere necessities trying to hold on. Eventually he became homeless and found himself sleeping on a friend's couch dreaming of moving to Hawaii where he could finally relax.

A year or so later he finally declared bankruptcy and took what little he had and bought a plane ticket to Maui. Within a short while he was working as grounds manager of a beachfront condominium, where he lived and was enjoying some peace and freedom. He soon started overseeing a large construction project for a friend and the last time we visited him he was living temporarily in the 14million dollar home he was now caring for. He was awaiting the completion of his own waterfront cottage which he could hardly wait to be completed as he was so uncomfortable being in the grandeur of the big house. I remember floating in the invisible edge swimming pool, which practically dripped over into the Pacific Ocean, laughing at how we all resist being completely worthy.

My friend Jim was a perfect example. Here is a man who loves people, gave up a very promising sports career when he went to fight for his country in Viet Nam, he would give anyone the shirt off his own back, and yet he struggles receiving gifts and love from others.

With all the resistance he put up I couldn't help but notice how Spirit was still managing to flood his life with abundance, giving him every opportunity to work through being the worthiness of God, who clearly he is!

We are saying that owning our Divinity, being the worthiness of Spirit is essential to being abundance. However our unworthiness shows up (our own personal version of "not enough.") We have practiced that way of being and our life is an expression of that.

See it didn't matter whether I was sleeping on the couch in my children's apartment in the Mission District or swimming in Hawaii what I had to attend to was where I was putting my attention.

There was a time in the early nineties when the clothing business that Jeanne (my first wife) and I had was heavily in debt and on the verge of defaulting. We had thirty employees and I couldn't see how I could keep making payroll much longer. Most of our employees were seam-stresses; they were our friends with car payments and mortgages. How was I going to look them in the eye and say, "I have no money?" I was desperate.

I remember thinking if I could just walk away from all this with my family and call it even, I gladly would. I was agonized by the possi-bility of defaulting on friends and family. The song, "*I'm a Loser*" was blaring in my head. I felt backed into a corner facing failure, shame, and embar-rassment. I was desperately seeking to alter my outer circumstances as if my suffering were out there.

Then I had an insight. I saw I was not my circumstance; I *had* circumstances. It was like I was looking in the mirror at my self and I didn't like the image I saw.

I had been trying to change the image by drawing on the mirror but all the suf-fering was over here with me. I saw the futility of this, I felt cornered and suddenly I let go of having to prove a thing. I saw that the only thing separating me from loving my life was the unworthiness I clung to. With my ego suffi-ciently squashed I chose to surrender to a love, the unswerving love a mother has for a child. I got out of the way and let the Divine love itSelf as me. I was flooded with peace. I re-membered something I had been taught and started saying it to myself.

I am adoring myself,
I am adoring
everyone else,
I am the adoring
love of God,
Radiating for myself
and all.

Soon after I experienced this new freedom I received a phone call from a **total stranger** that loved our clothing. She introduced me to a friend who was interested in the possibility of becoming involved in our business. That friend extended me the money for the upcoming payroll and later became our part-ner. He was instrumental in growing the business more then five fold in the next five years.

Most of us have had experi-ences like this and yet we resist surrendering to lov-ing and being loved all the time. We argue for our own unworthiness over and

"How can we send the highest love to others if we do not have it for ourselves."
Prentice Mulford

"I have an everyday religion that works for me, love yourself first and everything else falls in to place."
Lucille Ball

The clamor in my head is not I. I am that which is observing that less than honoring dialogue about me. Being worthy is honor-

over again. We think we are our failures and we carry those experiences of failing with us limiting our experience of abundance. Imagine if you surrendered to being the worthiness of Spirit what might be possible rather than defending to your death how unworthy you are?

ing one's self as Spirit and honoring Spirit as one's self. How silly that we are enslaved by fixing, changing, criticizing, and judging God's creation as our selves. Being worthy is the experiment of loving and accepting ourselves as we embrace the color of the sky and seeing what shows up. I encourage you to lavish yourself with the praise you reserve for a newborn babe.

In our practice on the days that the focus is on the WORTH current there will be mirror work to practice. You simply stand in front of the mirror and say kind, loving, supportive things to yourself (to the person in the mirror). When Matthew and I started practicing this I could hardly stand still and look at myself, my internal criticisms and

judgments got louder and louder. I could feel the internal battle of a lifetime; my arsenal of personal inadequacy was firing rapidly. I was embarrassed and ashamed.

Now there are days I can dance while I'm being with the person in the mirror, something I could never have imagined. I remember one day at yoga, I noticed my old pattern of looking in the mirror and critically comparing myself to everyone else surfacing, I caught myself and took on what I had been practicing instead. I looked directly at my own image and silently said, "I am adoring myself, I am adoring everyone else, I am the adoring love of God radiating for myself and all!" I immediately felt victorious. I could actually experience some freedom from the old and familiar competitive criticisms.

How wonderful it felt to be creating love for others and myself. This was something I had always wanted, I think most of us do, and I had just entertained over time judgmental, comparative and competitive thoughts.

One day we were playing our game THE ABOUNDING RIVER with some friends who were visiting the farm; I drew a card that said "Share something with the other players about your finances that you don't want to share." I said, "I still withdraw when people say, Matthew and Terces own the farm. I notice I have a hard time owning that, like somehow I don't deserve it, it isn't really mine, I just help

Matthew with it." My ego certainly has me do otherwise.

One way to tell where there is something to transform, to own up to, is look for what is the biggest stretch for you–for your identity. See here I am, I own the farm and I can't own it! It isn't out there; it's with me, with my unworthiness! This is why we say being worthy; the worthiness of Spirit is essential to being abundance.

How can we receive all the gifts of the Divine if we can't love our Self?

What's an example in your life, where you aren't owning what you have already been given? Remember we are *worthy* of everything wonderful!

Can you just let go and accept what is?

Love Acceptance

The Love Acceptance current is about bestowing being to EVERYTHING!

Spirit gave us the freedom to show up anyway, business man, lecher, oil baron, terrorist, drug addict, dictator, saint, guru, couch potato, etc.

Ego refuses to extend the same courtesy to the world that Spirit extends to us. We will argue that something is wrong, that life isn't great because of something out there.

We criticize some other way Spirit is expressing as being not Spirit- not part of *one* working whole. We analyze and resist how Spirit is expressing and this keeps us separate, alone, disempowered, timid, and not present to wholeness or abundance.

By not accepting the whole of life as Spirit, we create for others and ourselves a world separate from ourselves to defend against, hoard against, and protect against. Every time we have a thought, speech, belief, action, or attitude of "something's missing or wrong," we add another brick to the paradigm of scarcity, we cast our vote for the dichotomy of us and them, good and evil. When we sow fear in our wake the rest of us dig in to defend.

"Love is the reduction of the universe to a single being."
Victor Hugo

"The desire and pursuit of the whole is called love."
Plato

"The Great way is not difficult if you don't cling to good and bad. Just let go of your opinions and everything will be clear."

Third Zen Patriarch

"Every thought you have contributes to truth or illusion, it either extends the truth or multiplies illusions."

A Course in Miracles

I have a sister, whom I love very much. She is an alcoholic and for years I have missed being able to really share and be close with her.

I have tried to fix her, change her, get her to stop drinking, encourage her to drink in front of me if she is going to drink, ignore it, ignore her, you name it I've tried it.

We drifted further and further apart as I really didn't want to be with her. One day when I was really listening to my inner wisdom I just "knew" I was to offer to go to Nashville with her and support her in putting on the rehearsal dinner for her eldest son's wedding. Miraculously she accepted and we set about planning the event together.

Although there were times when I experienced her as lost in an alcoholic stupor I was somehow able to just love and accept her, I experienced compassion for the anxiety, fear and trepidation she was dealing with.

In the midst of all the preparations she was up one night late watching television and saw a program about anxiety disorders and immediately identified with it. She ordered the tape program they offered and shared with me all about it the next day, that was the beginning of her recovery.

Can you consider that we don't see the whole picture? Consider that our egos cannot see nor have any interest in the perfection of an over-all plan. In the context of eternal Spirit rousing creation to know it Self, what seems like madness now may have value in the long view.

The African slave trade seems heinous by contemporary standards and I am not minimizing its horrors but without the transatlantic traffic of slaves there would be no Jazz, no Gospel music, no Langston Hughes, no Maya Angelou, no Willie Mays...

Had there been no religious intolerance in Europe there would be no Quakers to birth Pennsylvania, no Irving Berlin or George Gershwin, no Bob Dylan, no Werner Erhard, no mystical sixties, no yoga at the Y.M.C.A.

The Roman Empire was a severe tyranny for many of its citizens and surely most Romans couldn't appreciate that tyranny as part of the evolution of consciousness. But two thousand years later one can see the progression of events that join us with the sensibilities of antiquity. One possible interpretation is that without Rome there is no Christmas Story, no growth of the early church, no Reformation, no exodus to the new world, no democracy influenced by the Iroquois Confederacy, no Bill Of Rights, no cultural melting pot, no Lutherans from Cedar Rapids adopting Chinese baby girls.

What part of history is not part of us? We are the blessings of our ancestors; their experiences and trials are gifts to us. We invite you to give up resisting the past and the present and experiment with accepting what is. Perhaps in fifty years the consensus may sneer in disdain, "The people of 2004 actually allowed Coca Cola vending machines in schools, imprisoned farmers for growing marijuana, cut down the rain forest for the production of beef and managed their children with Prozac and television."

Perhaps in 100 years people will look at the movies from this era and be bewildered that human beings actually passed one another on the street without making eye contact or acknowledging one another.

I often look at my personal life if I want to get present to the ever-forwarding flow of consciousness. My divorce after 22 years of marriage was very painful at the time but now I can see that the grief I experienced was a doorway to emotions I was unwilling to experience. Spirit was nudging me to embrace my humanity and I was left freer to be more intimate.

The circumstances of our lives are the boulders in the current of Spirit directing us in the optimum direction. Spirit is always stretching us to experience more of it Self, more possibility of being more Spirit- more love, more joy, more abundance. Spirit always intends us to recognize it Self, our Self. The system is perfect.

We begin to resist life when we can't conceive that we are the source of our experience. We start judging when we can't see that what is happening now is a golden opportunity- Spirit awakening to Spirit. Our deteriorating ecological situation is a perfect example of this.

I tend to accuse unconscious consumers and big bad corporations for being in in bed with corrupt politicians. This blame game invokes in me anger and powerlessness along with the sense of being surrounded by a world so scary that I'm ready to bail out to Hawaii and become a survivalist. This has me experience being separate, alone, and dwelling in scarcity.

Now consider our ecological crisis in terms of One Body having us become conscious that we are all connected, inseparable from the earth and each other. There is no taking care of just ourselves any more. We are being guided to take care of each other and the earth as One, as the One Spirit Family we are.

Thank God for the awakening our global crisis provides.

I just read *Fast Food Nation* by Eric Schlosser. It is a muckraker expose' about the fast food industry. I gave myself the experience of disgust and directed it at large multi-national corporations. "How can *they* be so greedy?" I thought.

Then I saw that my anger was a smoke screen. Those corporations are comprised of human beings stuck in survival, trying to accumulate wealth to protect themselves against others trapped in the same game. Those corporations also have corporate egos scurrying around intent on surviving.

We built those corporations one burger, one car, and one gallon of gas at a time. We voted them into existence with *our* dollars chasing some life *out there*.

Where are we going? The notion that it is better there then here is a source of greed and dissatisfaction.

Who can we be to shift the worldview from one of lack and eternally getting somewhere to a culture

that savors being present to all there already is? Where are we participating in the illusion of, *"I'll be happy when...?"*

We can resist how life is with our judgments and analyses but then we are held captive by our opinions. What we can't accept owns us. We can make some entity wrong or we can look and see where we can extend our self.

How can we be more honoring of the whole of which we are part? In what ways are we not attentive to the Whole? What part of Spirit is Spirit stretching us to love and contribute to?

We will realize that we are **all** Spirit- the curriculum is mandatory. Spirit will allow us to trash our bodies, our planet, Spirit's body, and Spirit's planet in order that we get who we are.

Our point is we are awakening to what we have always been. Spirit is doing a great job awakening all its parts. *God really is handling it.* What would our day-to-day experience be if we really trusted life?

"There is nothing wrong with God's creation. Misery and suffering only exist in the mind."
Ramana Maharshi

"True affluence is not needing anything."
Gary Snyder

Ego loves to judge and assess God's creation. Imagine in your own body if your kidneys were perturbed by your slouchy stomach and so decided they were only going to love and serve the rest of the body when they felt like it. Imagine that they now claim to be independent and not responsible for your body's health. What would that be like for the kidneys? What about the whole system? We cannot be separate! We can complain and moan and create the illusion of being separate and endure the suffering that separation fosters but eventually we **will** gain the awareness of what has always been so.

There is only *One of Us*.

We believe it is from this view of oneness that the Dalai Lama can create the Chinese invasion of Tibet as a contribution to a renaissance of Tibetan culture. He considers these events as an opportunity to hone the Tibetians practice of Buddhism.

While this declaration is neither popular, verifiable, or easy, it places him as a part of a whole, responsible for all of it, unhindered by blame or regret and free to extend love.

Try as a practice incorporating every event in life as a perfect awakening for the parts involved, whether it is your divorce or an act of violence on the other side of the world. Sleeping souls are waking up; the parts are understanding they must act with consideration of the whole, sometimes with great resistance,

"The entire law is summed up in a single command, love thy neighbor as thy self."

Galatians 5:14

"Seeing difference is ignorance."

Shankara

"There are no others."

Ramana Maharshi

"You judge according to the flesh, I judge no one."

John 8:15

I am a proponent of living foods. I believe the best way to nourish our bodies is by eating the freshest most vibrant raw foods available. Imagine if I sought to introduce live foods to the public school system in America. How will I be received if I have the attitude that the administration, the parents, the cafeteria workers, THE SYSTEM is wrong and the people ignorant? Their only option is to dig in and fight for their position because I've created another separate position. I've triggered their ego already in a constant state of threat. Let's consider a different path: now visualize me approaching the educators as with a gift that I am sharing with a reputable team. Now I have a chance to be heard.

There is nothing wrong with our judgments and opinions. They are all reminders that ego is doing the driving, that we have moved our attention from the body of life working as one whole to a lone surviving gunslinger. Our judgments are all opportunities to *Spiritize*, to think, speak, believe, act and attitude as

Love- the state of Spirit recognizing it Self. In our Abounding River workshop many people who have attended express concern that if they or people in general just accept everything, nothing would get done, passivity would reign, the world would fall apart, as if their judgments were what fuels their actions. Does a mother have to see something wrong to feed a child? Can't we plant a tree as a self-expression of beauty and not as a reaction to a perceived threat? Consider that our judgments, assessments, and opinions exonerathe ego's scary "something's wrong" "somewhere to get" world which drowns out our ability to hear where Spirit (the voice of the Whole) would have us serve, have us love next.

One day while we were working on this book, Henri, a friend of ours, asked us, "Just when are you going to open up this Café you keep talking about anyway?" Matthew replied, "As soon as God shows us the perfect place." The next day we were driving home from the farmer's market and we saw a sign that read, "Restaurant Available," on a building right in front of us. We jotted down the phone number, drove home and called.

We looked at some pictures of the place on the Internet and couldn't believe how wonderful it all looked. Even though we felt guided and acknowledged the speed at which a building showed up and the perfection of it all, our egos still played games with us. "Oh let's just see if the board game fits on the table tops," the voice in our heads shouted! We were the first people to look at the building and the owner took an immediate liking to us. Not only was the space perfect for our vision, but there stacked up against one wall were some uncommonly large wooden tables that turned out to be the exact size we wanted for the game boards.

The day we took possession of the building, Bill, a general contractor friend of ours, called to say he was driving through San Francisco and

would love to stop by. We told him we were on the way to the Café to pick up the keys so he said he'd meet us there. Because of perfect timing, Bill was there to take a photo of us getting the keys from the previous owner. Discovering that he had a six week break before his next project, we invited him to move in with us to head up the remodel, which he gladly did. Now Matthew and I keep reminding ourselves, "God's handling it."

Love and Acceptance entails trusting Spirit, trusting your Self, trusting that the Universe (the one song) is working as One. Love Acceptance is trusting that God loves its Creation and is doing a great job awakening all the cells of God's body.

Love-Acceptance is trusting that death isn't real- that life is eternal.

Here is a Zen Koan that sums up the Love \ Acceptance current:

The Seeker

A man left his home and family to seek the Truth. In a far away land in a village market he overheard a conversation between a baker and his customer. "Give me the best loaf of bread you have," said the customer. "Everything in my stall is the best," replied the baker. "You cannot find here any loaf that is not the best." At these words the seeker was home.

There is a whole world working together on our behalf

Gratitude

Gratitude is one of the most powerful currents. Gratitude puts our being in the shape of having. There is a **Whole Creation** working as One Body for It Self, for us. How much of our day is our attention on thanksgiving? How much of our day is our attention on "something's missing?"

Gratitude breaks down the barriers of separation. We get out of ego; we are rescued from a recurrent when we are being grateful (great-full). Being grateful expands our world. Every religion and spiritual discipline incorporates the practice of gratitude. Being grateful is a practice.

One day I walked into a café and ordered a tuna fish sandwich. When the sandwich was set in front of me I had an epiphany. A whole creation arose, the universe of this tuna sandwich. All at once I could see: the tuna fleet, the diesel mechanics, the net makers, the hook makers, the crew and their families, the cannery, the can maker, the baker, the wheat farmer, the combine mechanic, the grain elevator operator, the wheat geneticist, the lettuce grower, the chicken farmer, countless bankers, secretaries and receptionists, truck drivers, then the earthworms, the soil microorganisms, the food chain of the oceans, the plankton, herring, mackerel- all placed before me for $4.50. I saw the whole body of creation working twenty-four hours, seven days a week to support our existence without our attention. We don't have to manage a thing! I don't have call out, "Don't forget to bring the hooks." Most of the time we're oblivious to the orchestration of the cosmos and in the dense oblivion of ingratitude we'll question the existence of God or complain about the price of a sandwich.

"A thankful heart is not only the greatest virtue but the parent of all the other virtues."   *Cicero*

"Man's chief work is to praise God."
                Augustine

"Who does not thank for little will not thank for much."
        Estonian Proverb

"Human beings have almost an infinite capacity for taking things for granted."
        Aldous Huxley

54

"The person who has stopped being thankful has fallen asleep in life."

Robert Louis Stevenson

A master and a few disciples were walking along a road. They came upon a dead dog, putrid, bloated, and full of maggots. One of the disciples cried out, "Oh Master, how terrible." *"Beautiful white teeth,"* said the master.

Earlier this year someone broke into our home during the night while we were sleeping. They stole our audio-visual equipment as well as our car keys and car!

I remember when we awoke for yoga early the next morning and discovered the robbery I immediately experienced being GRATEFUL that we hadn't awakened, heard something and come downstairs. My attention wasn't on anything else.

I also noticed when the police, the insurance representative, and then the detective came; who took fingerprints, all we experienced was gratitude. We were amazed at how many different people and organizations there were working on our behalf to resolve the matter.

Matthew and I commented for weeks on how our families and friends seemed more upset about the loss and violation of our private space than we did. We were too busy immersing ourselves in gratitude.

Look and see if there isn't always something to be grateful for and to acknowledge. We are surrounded by a remarkable creation that we mostly take for granted. When we give ourselves over to and relish what we already have our lives are full beyond measure and we nurture the miraculous. When we focus on what is missing the amnesia of scarcity sets in. *Remembering how fortunate we are is a magic wand.*

We have all heard many times that we often don't appreciate what we have until it's gone; well this is an opportunity to appreciate all you have right NOW. Especially when you think you have very little!

This is also a wonderful way to interrupt the ego when it has a hold on you, to intervene in a scarcity experience, simply start putting your attention on what you are grateful for (we suggest three or more things).

On the Abounding River we call this a *lifeline.* Preferably share with

There is always something to be grateful for.

someone else what you are grateful for. Start being a gratitude sleuth and really stretch yourself, start acknowledging and being grateful for forms of supply you have never before recognized: parks, hot water, street cleaning, garbage pick-up, borrowing your friend's tools, someone buying you coffee, good roads, clean air, farmers markets, the trees on your street, your health, other peoples health, public rest rooms...

We challenge you, we request of you, make your life about being grateful, make a game of it, ask everyone you meet, "What are you grateful for?" Turn it up when you hear complaining.

Ask people who leave a message for you on your answering machine to include one thing they are grateful for, ask the telemarketers who call you, ask a homeless person.

Watch your life dissolve into the awe and fullness of every moment and your being shift from getting and doing to being fulfilled.

I went to Lithuania shortly after the fall of the Soviet Union looking for fabric and a sewing factory for our production. In the fall of 1992, the Baltic States were emerging from a deep economic slumber; there was no heat, no hot water, and no fresh food, especially for a vegetarian.

I remember being served frozen cabbage salad for breakfast. While it was the beginning of life-long friendships and an extraordinary mutually benefiting

57

relationship, that first trip was like visiting a kingdom of resignation, void of light and smiles and fifty years behind the times.

Perhaps the cultural attitude was best summed up by my friend Regina's response to this question, "Aren't you concerned about nuclear power?" (Chernobyl was fresh on my mind.) "Life isn't so good here, we don't want to live so long," she said.

After ten days I returned to New York late at night and early the next morning I headed up to Massachusetts. As I drove along the Brooklyn-Queens expressway with Manhattan on my left the sun rose and illuminated all the glass of the skyscrapers. I began to weep and continued to be moved by waves of gratitude all the way up the Taconic Parkway.

I had fallen asleep to all I had in my life and how much I loved our country. I had become sedated by my circumstances. At the time I was $250,000 in debt and had two failing businesses. Living on a hope and a prayer I had bought my ticket to Lithuania with my last morsel of credit.

Now I was awakened to my real wealth. Abundance is only now, gratitude is an access to experiencing abundance, and outer circumstances are extraneous.

Who would Spirit deny?

Generosity

As we were creating the illustrations with Frank for the Generosity Current we noticed we had fallen into the routine of feeding the homeless people in our neighborhood, and realized it was no longer a stretch for us, as we suggest in the practice of being generous. Matthew said, "You know the illustration on the Generosity card indicates that a woman is inviting someone on the streets into her home? Why don't we do that?" We both agreed that would be a stretch!

The next day we pulled up next to a collection of shopping carts and bundles and saw a woman named Jason whom we had previously fed. We asked her if she would like to come to our home for a bath. She said, "I would love to, but not today; How about tomorrow at 3pm?" She explained that her husband had been arrested and that she couldn't leave all their belongings.

We said, "Sure," and drove off, both of us remarking to one another that in our imaginations if we lived on the streets and someone offered us a bath, we would jump at the chance!

We went by the next day at three o'clock and called out to Jason. She called back from her tent formation, "I don't feel good today so I can't come; How about tomorrow at 2pm?" she asked. Once again we said, "Sure," and drove off.

The next day we arrived at 2pm and she apologized, saying that it still wasn't going to work. However she promised it would work the following day if we could drop her recycling off at the recycling center where her son would meet us and then after her bath take her to the food donation center at a nearby church. We said we could.

When we pulled up the following day she was on the curb waiting with her bags and boxes of recycling which she loaded into our van. She had a suitcase packed with clean clothes and as she climbed inside she handed us a picture of her daughter to look at. Jason shared with us all about her family who she was clearly proud of. She also told us about her last job where she worked for years as a counselor for the homeless, helping to find ways for them to get off the streets.

At the recycling center she unloaded her bags and boxes with the help of her son, who was there waiting for us on a bicycle. She

explained that he was going to wait in line for his turn to get money for the cans and bottles, while she came with us. On our way to the house she continued to tell us about how living on the streets she had lost weight at last, had more time to read, and had a great community of friends who share and look out for one another.

She also said they were saving up money to get a room at a residential hotel. She said she missed her daughter, however was so grateful that she got to visit her every week or so and watch TV with her in her room. She was a little worried about her son. By now we were later than we had planned and Matthew and I left her in the bathtub while we ran out to do a couple of errands.

When we got back the bathroom door was still shut and we called to Jason to let her know we only had fifteen more minutes before we needed to leave for an appointment. She said she would be ready. In just a few moments Jason

emerged, clean clothes, washed and combed hair, and she had scrubbed the bathroom spotless with some cleaning supplies she had brought with her. She thanked us very much as she loaded her suitcase in the car and we headed for the food bank to drop her off.

This current is a bit more elusive than you might think. Most of us when we think about being generous, we experience it in the form of doing something for someone else. Often times this is someone we perceive as needing help, food, clothes, etc.

While that is great, that is not what we are referring to here. Generosity, as we are distinguishing it, is simply opening up to the flow, being in the flow, going with the current.

If your hands are full, you can't hold more. If your lungs are full, you can't take in more air.

Generosity is living and being the consciousness that releasing and receiving are one and the same. Generosity is sharing money and forms of supply like we share the air we breathe.

There is no more need *over there* or more worthy *over here*. Everybody is somebody's mother, father, daughter or son. Generosity is being we are One.

Generosity is attending to our ever-expanding experience of the Whole. It is not deciding who is in need, or whose cause is worthy.

Generosity does not consist of scrutinizing, by asking, "What are they going to do with the money?" Generosity is none of that. Whom would Spirit deny? Who are we to deny Spirit as the homeless man, the government, the N.R.A or the N.O.W.? Wouldn't you feed your father regardless of his politics? This is being the benevolence of Spirit as your life.

In the winter of 1994 I was in Lithuania overseeing clothing production for our company. One night we were sharing a hotel sauna with some Californian doctors who were in the Baltic States performing free cataract surgeries.

They had arrived ill clothed for the Lithuanian winter and were having a hard time keeping warm. We were manufacturing sweaters at the time and I offered to give them a box full of sweaters to stave off the cold. They were very thankful and when I inquired about their practices in the States one of them told me about his corrective eye surgery practice.

I asked him how much the procedure would cost me.

He said, "A box of sweaters". When I returned to the U.S., I had the $3,000 surgery performed on my eyes.

Our practice of generosity is enjoying the giving and receiving of supply. We experience generosity by allowing money and the forms of supply to pass through our lives without clinging to it.

In our practice money is shared like breath or hugs or smiles. *We are creating money as a sacrament.* Every time we pass along supply we have the opportunity to presence Spirit; to

"Nothing less than becoming one with the universe will suffice."

Morihei Uyeshisba

emanate, "Hey, this is a plentiful Spiritual world, I'm glad to be sharing it with you."

By being generous we vanquish scarcity and we "build our muscle" in surrender and trust.

Begin noticing **who** you are being the moment money passes your hands, for example, the moment you write a check, or when- ever you use your credit card.

Are you present to connecting and contributing to thousands of lives? Are you aware of what the grocery clerk provides for you and what you provide him or her? Do you make present the **whole body** that you are part of with the coffee vendor, and the mechanic?

When you pay your phone bill imagine a blue haired woman living in a mobile home in central Florida getting her dividend check from the phone company that you participated in. Visualize her going out and buying her granddaughter a rain stick made in a village in central Mexico. With

rain stick funds the village buys a new water pump and the pump manufacturer uses software designed by your friend who took you out for dinner last week.

Money is a body fluid linking us all together. Money is an expression of Spirit and abundance (SpiritAbundance) flowing through us, connecting us all. When you deny the flow to some part of the whole body you are cutting yourself off.

Several years ago I felt spiritually nudged to give almost everything away. My family thought I was crazy. My Mother wanted me to give her back anything of sentimental value so she could keep those items for me until this phase passed, so I would still have them.

I remember the freedom and joy I felt as people arrived at our home and began taking items they wanted. The local newspaper had run an article about the give away and several non-profit organizations had come. It was a wonderful experience.

Some years later after traveling for nearly a year we settled into the redwoods in Northern California and in less than two years I was funded by a customer in a café where I worked for starting my own business and was moving into a 10,000 square foot warehouse which was quickly filled with equipment, desks, chairs, plants, carpets, couches, tables, mirrors, all contributed by others!

This was a great experience in releasing and receiving. You may have had an experience like this, and you may know it isn't easy to stay this fluid. It takes practice to be unattached.

One day while playing the Abounding River Game, I drew a card that read, "With whom are you stingy? Whom would you deny?" Because of this card Matthew and I started to contribute to every organization or individual who made a request of us for one month.

It didn't matter what the amount; we simply made a contribution. Paying the bills became a whole new

experience for me; I was moved by how many organizations there were in the world committed to supporting something.

This practice eliminated any tendency we had to judge, approve or disapprove and gave us the opportunity to simply release, to be in the flow.

Our tip in this current is, *if you aren't relishing something, release it*. This will support you in practicing being generous.

Throughout my life I have contributed to others, and although I would make beautiful and thoughtful gifts for family and friends, when I thought of myself as being generous I was usually giving something to someone who I perceived as having less than I or needing something I could share or contribute, though this may be generous, it is not the gernerosity we are practicing.

In our practice being generous is simply releasing into the flow, letting go. Certainly letting go of items you aren't relishing now: clothes you no

"All you are unable to give, possesses you."
Andre Gide

longer wear or belongings stored in basements and storage units. You may still love these things; they may even have sentimental value. If however you aren't using them now they are stuck energy and are clogging the flow.

In our workshop we do an exercise which involves everyone starting with some amount of money they are willing to share with the rest of the group. It really doesn't matter what the denomination is. Then we stand in a circle and for one minute "give away" as much money as we can as quickly as we can. If at any time we have no money, we just put our hands out, palms up. The money moves around the circle quickly and the energy level is high. Everyone is laughing and smiling. The internal chatter of the ego disappears. Everyone experiences being connected, being part of one whole.

Then for the next minute everyone is to "hold on to" whatever amount of money he or she has, squeezes it tight, doesn't let it go. The energy in the room goes flat; participants have a difficult time even looking at one another; every one experiences being separate and alone. The noise in our heads is screaming.

The interesting thing is in both parts of the exercise the amount of money is the same, yet our experience of the money is dramatically different. Consider that the world operates in just the same way.

"Love everybody, serve everybody, remember God."
Neem Karoli Baba

Where does money go anyway?

Abundance

This is the knowingness of being always completely supplied. We know the sun is going to rise, we are sure there is going to be fruit on the trees in the fall; we don't wonder if the grass will be growing in the spring, we never question these future events.

Imagine experiencing the same conviction, the same assurance of being supplied. Practicing that kind of certainty is the being of abundance.

Being abundance is surren- dering your ego's obsession with fixing life on the altar of this now moment. Being abundance is being that life turned out, that we are rich, that nothing is miss- ing, that there is nowhere to get- *now*.

Look at reality. Abundance permeates us, we are

swimming in it and mostly we miss it. A world of plenty is obscured by our scarcity colored glasses.

If you are an American, by virtue of your citizenship alone you are already on the upper tier of the first class cabin of the planet earth. There are at least 5 billion people who would gladly trade your American experience of affluence for theirs.

How many of us have ever missed a meal, not had a place to sleep, not had access to drinking water or hot water? Where is there evidence that you are lack- ing anything? What has God failed to provide? Where is your attention?

We sell out on the truth of our abundance when we worry about making our car payment, unconsciously forgetting that just having a car to pay for puts us in the privileged 5% bracket of the entire population of the planet.

Can you see you are always being provided for?

"While you fear missing a meal, you aren't fully aware of the meals you do eat."
Dan Millman

"Wise men count their blessings, fools their problems."
Anonymous

"Enough is as good as a feast."
John Heywood

"Nothing is enough to a man for whom enough is too little."
Epicurus

There are places on earth where having a good well within a mile of one's home is considered a luxury. We are not attempting to elicit guilt and shame here. We are making a point about how we as human beings fall asleep.

I had the privilege of hosting many Lithuanians in the United States soon after the fall of the Soviet Union. For most of their lives they had waited in line for hours for the opportunity to buy a coveted jar of mayonnaise, shoes that didn't fit, toilet paper, items we in America don't even think about as we grab them off the shelves of our aptly named supermarkets.

The overwhelming gratitude and joy these Lithuanians experienced in their first western grocery was very moving. My Lithuanian friend Regina recalls having heard a rumor during the Soviet years that in America toilet paper was available in a variety of colors. She was certain it was a lie. A few years later she was matching toilet tissue to her new bathroom tile.

All the basic necessities are now available in Lithuania and the new world of plenty has become nearly transparent to them in just a few years. Yesterday's abundance is today's "not enough."

This is no different from what can happen in a relationship over time, if we on don't lucidly appreciate our partner's magnificence. At some point ego will dwell on what's missing, what isn't working. I fell in love with my first wife because she was in my eyes an artistic free spirit. I perceived with the passing of time the exact same person as self-centered and irresponsible.

In one of our workshops someone was complaining about how their problems really were about not having enough; they felt like we just didn't understand how little they had, they wanted our life.

We listened and then asked them: "What if everyone in the entire world, all six billion of us, put our name on a ping pong ball and threw it into a big hopper. Everyone now gets a chance to pick out a ball and take that person's life. Would you put your name on a ball and toss it in?"

Suddenly the person said, "No Way!" With this new perspective he now began to see how fortunate he was. Most of us live a completely abundant life, only our attention is on what's missing and we are afraid of losing what we already have. Being abundant is keeping our attention on what has already been given; in so doing a whole new experience of life begins to show up.

We are swimming in massive abundance just as we are swimming in love or any other quality of Spirit. In reality Spirit provides profusely but when we are identified with our ego's survival tale we are asleep to all we have and we are reinforcing the habit of scarcity. If we are still insatiable even after dining sumptuously in the first class cabin, what chance do our brothers and sisters in steerage have?

At our workshops people often ask, "What about the impoverished, the third world, the hopeless? How can they be abundance? In response we ask that the person first looks to see if each can perceive and own that they are abundance now and always. If you can't embrace that you are provided for, you surely can't see that possibility in the lives of others.

Remember that when the Europeans came to North America they "saw" destitute heathens living in bark huts and a whole continent going to waste. We can ask ourselves, how reliable are our evaluations? How trustworthy are our senses for that matter? Consider we can't always see how Spirit is working in and as others.

I've known drug addicts who transformed their lives and started being responsible only after really tasting the gutter. I couldn't always see or trust their process because I was blinded by their circumstances.

"There is no greater hell then doubts."
Amar Joyti

My friend's husband ran off with her best friend. She lived in deep emotional despair for perhaps a year; now that formerly bitter woman is able to recognize that her former husband is her liberator.

Must we always analyze every situation? Let's try being in a condition of **not knowing** as a possibility. **This is a faith experiment.** What does it provide the world or yourself to evaluate according to a cramped yardstick concocted by your ego? What would be available if you trusted life's process?

Notice all the forms of supply (food, money, shelter, entertainment, borrowed items, a friends help, street cleaning, etc) you received in the last 48 hours. Some you paid for; some landed in your lap. Look over your life and notice how Spirit has always provided regardless of the obstacles you put in the way. Get present to all you have in your life.

Being abundance is being rich *now*. WE ARE RICH, we are love, we are joy. The fact that we don't experience the quality of being rich has no validity because we've allowed circumstances to determine our experience.

Our ego self is a detective on par with Sherlock Holmes: it is a habitual sleuth for scarcity and will always have us come up short even as we are drowning in supplies.

Not enough money, not enough love, not enough sex, not enough time, blah-blah-blah.

Our Spirit Self, which we can always access instantly and be present to in our thoughts, speech, beliefs, actions and attitudes, is whole and complete.

Being abundance is the exquisite experiment of living life from inside out. Being abundant is being fulfilled now and graciously receiving what is given again and again.

Through your awareness of the abundance that is already present you will receive more than you can ever imagine but remember not to expect it to look any particular way. Specific egocentric expectations reduce our experience of joy in life and limit Spirit's palette. We can trust that Spirit is always providing the best for it Self as us.

In my case I was given a very successful business. Not only did wealth beyond my wildest dreams flow into my life, but I was able to create jobs for hundreds, perhaps thousands, of people. I set up a woman-run worker-owned sewing factory in Lithuania and supported two large linen producers so they could upgrade, and thereby sell to the world market.

I relished what I received and was enamored by the goodies. I bought properties, lived like a king, shared it, always picked up the tab, and kept the dollars in circulation. I had bouts of doubt that the wealth was a result of who I was being.

The bank balance was huge but my experience of security was still a roller coaster. Many times I continued to measure my sense of well-being by the bank balance. Money, like everything in outer life (beauty, houses, cars, stuff) is very alluring, glamorous, and sticky.

Spirit is like an old farmer that never wastes a motion, for whom every action has a purpose.

Spirit is interested in recognizing it Self, in seeing that I recognize that I am Abundance (or any other Spirit quality) regardless of

circumstances. Spirit expressed as my divorce, the sale of the my business, lawsuits, property values declining, loss of assets, etc so I could understand that abundance is actually and really, a state of Being.

Thank you, Spirit, thank you. I forgot I am not my checking account balance."

I now know at a deeper level that I am abundance and that abundance can look **anyway**. If Terces and I were living in our camper, we would be being abundance.

In my case I was given more than all I ever wanted; the love of my life and abundance beyond anything I could have imagined.

Once I finally surrendered, let go and truly trusted, there was someone I dearly love who loves me, and the coming together of families I had always dreamed was possible.

I was a single mother for nearly 15 years, with a few close friends working hard to *make it on my own,* constantly struggling with a sense of unworthiness that seemed embedded in my core. When it came to money and material resources I always felt inadequate and was trying to figure out how to make more.

That is what my life looked like, lots of opportunities to make more, in other words always chasing some proverbial carrot. Only when I started being worthy and creating what I had as the best did my world shift. Suddenly I was part of a loving and generous community. There were 250 friends and family members at our wedding.

"If you count all your assets you always show a profit."
Robert Quillen

"Lay up yourselves treasures in heaven, where neither moth nor rust destroys and where thieves do not break in and steal." *Matthew 6:20*

"Better a hand full with quietness than both hands full together with toil and grasping for the wind."   *Ecclesiastes*

It is fine to come to this practice looking for more money. You shall indeed have more. Please remember though that when you make your life about the outer effect, when you get too enamored by the stuff, you will reveal to yourself that abundance is not **out there**; it is the nectar of your being.

Just behind the curtain of surrender is that which we have always been, shall always be, and that which we want to experience more than all else.

Oranges are an expression or out-picturing of the being of orange tree. Kisses and hugs are an expression or an out-picturing of love; they are not love any more then oranges are orange trees.

One can give out kisses and hugs and not have the

experience of love and one can have lots of money and the forms of supply and not experience abundance. The outer effect is no guarantee. But if one is being love, one may share kisses and hugs all day long and love will never be diminished.

There is an Indian saint named Ammachi, whose mission in the world is to hug people. We have seen her in the early morning after hugging people all night. Being anchored in love, she is as fresh and present with the first person she hugs as with the last.

Money (and all forms of supply) and abundance have the same relationship that hugs and kisses have to love. Consider that we all could circulate money as we do authentic hugs and kisses, as the honoring

and celebration of Spirit. Consider money is just a symbol, an effect, an out-picturing of who we are being, of who Spirit is. Dollars are an effect of our awareness of ourselves as plentiful. Money is not itself abundance; money is one representation of the experience of abundance.

Imagine a world where the exchange of money evokes the presence of Spirit. Imagine if we wrote checks, shared dollars, used our credit cards, with the same love, the same conscious-ness as we do passing out photographs of a beloved.

To whom would we choose to give those photographs? To whom would we deny one? In giving away the pictures of our loved one is our experience of our beloved diminished or enhanced? Will we have any less by giving away those photos? Imagine thinking we had to hoard the photographs to con-tinue to experience our beloved. Imagine thinking the photographs were the source of love or security.

Most of us have money and abundance collapsed in the same way as we do *having* a relationship collapsed with love. Having a relationship is fantastic; it is an extraor-dinary opportunity. But is it a promissory note for love?

Having money is great but it guarantees nothing of substance. Notice how endless *having* is.

Notice how when you finally *get* that job, that car, that relationship, that vacation, that degree, there is ALWAYS somewhere, or something else to get. In the U.S. we have the highest standard of *having*.

"If one surrenders completely, there will be no one left to ask questions... Surrender can never be regarded as complete as long as the devotee wants this or that from God."
Ramana Maharshi

When we drove across the country recently we noticed at the edge of nearly every town we were greeted by acres of self-storage units. We have so much stuff and we keep wanting more!

This comes at the expense of spending time with our families, taking care of our health, participating in our communities, relaxing and enjoying ourselves, committing to a Spiritual practice, etc.

Is this really a picture of abundance realized? We're not diminishing all we have, but notice how all our *having*, our great material wealth, is not leaving us satisfied and fulfilled.

A man named Mark walked up to the register in Café Gratitude one day and requested our menu item called, "I am Open." I said, "Sure," and rang up the cup of Organic Earl Grey tea. "That will be $2.44," I said. As he handed me some

money, he asked, "Do you know you have the best Earl Grey in the city?" "I do know it's great," I replied handing him his change. I felt proud of our tea selection and happy that someone noticed.

He put some money in the tip jar and shared with me his experience of growing bergamot fruit and educating me on the difference the real fruit in tea makes compared to just the oil, or essence. Bergamot is the primary flavor of Earl Grey tea. I shared with him my experience of our Earl Grey and told him how proud I was of the teas we serve.

Later I looked up and noticed him thoroughly enjoying his hot cup of tea, both hands wrapped around the bowl-like cup we use for tea. Tears collected in my smiling eyes as I watched, so grateful for his appreciation. After all, that is what our café is about, people being present to how great their life is right now!

Later on that night on our way home, Matthew and I pulled up to someone sleeping on the streets to drop off some food we had brought with us. As we set it down beside a body cuddled inside a blanket, the person looked up and said, "Thank-you." Matthew and I were surprised as we looked into the eyes of the man who had come in for the cup of tea earlier that night.

As we headed home we both shared what a perfect example of being abundance Mark is. Here is someone sleeping on the streets who is happy to pay for the highest quality tea and even put the change in the tip jar!

When ego is allowed to drive, any moment, any circumstance will be reduced to some version of scarcity. Abundance is a *now* phenomenon. If you ever notice yourself trying to get to abundance, stop immediately and take notice of all you have. There is no *getting to* abundance. That is a false promise of your ego.

"Language is the house of being."
Martin Heidegger

We want you to consider that the language we traffic in day to day is not the most powerful for keeping our attention on abundance or Oneness any more than the language of the 19th century would be adequate to communicate and describe present-day computer science, psycho-therapy, physics, etc. Our inherited language is a language of separation. Part of the training we are offering is the opportunity to create in our speaking the reality that we, Spirit and abundance, are One.

Let's look at the power of language. Can you see that we are inundated with language from within and without; our conversations with ourselves, our conversations with others, listening to media, reading, etc. We are swimming in language and our moment-to-moment experience is largely driven by what our internal dialogue is saying about our life.

I have been meditating for 30 years. I have developed some ability to quiet my mind, to let my internal dialogue do it's thing and not identify with it. Yet still, plenty of my moment-to-moment experiences are a result of the interior conversation I am dwelling in.

Our thoughts are in language and from thoughts our experience arises. If you don't think language is so influential look at the impact it has on you when a parent, a spouse or a child withholds appreciation from you. What would your experience be if someone called you fat, or stupid, or ugly?

A friend called recently and shared with me the trials of her life and then said, "I just need a break." "A break from what?" I asked. Where can we go that will cause us to escape our internal dialogue, our on going conversation about our lives? That is what she really wanted a break from!

Part of this journey is to be more diligent and responsible for the language we use. We create our selves as shy, stupid, bored, lazy, unworthy, etc. in language, in the manner in which we speak. In language we can also create ourselves as expressions of Spirit.

Spirit is having a Matthew experience

We are going to create a language for ourselves that puts us at the source of our supply, that has us one with Spirit, one with abundance.

If I am just me, just that part of Spirit that identifies with this body and as Matthew, I'm speaking in such a way as separates me from a world out there, from Source, from abundance.

SpiritAbundanceMe is an example of the language of Oneness. *I am Spirit. Spirit is abundance. I am a bundance. No separation, one word.*

I struggled with this concept at first; it seemed so strange, as if I were speaking nonsense. Consider this is just like any other new language you might learn. When you first start to speak the words they sound foreign and unfamiliar, they are! However if you keep practicing or go to a country where that language is spoken you begin to become familiar and comfortable with the sounds and their meanings. It just takes practice.

I think my resistance was just more of my ego fighting for separation, fighting for what was familiar. Remember you are creating something *new*. Be patient with yourself.

Now you get to choose a SpiritAbundance Name for yourself.

In our workshops when participants begin to create a Spirit Abundance name for themselves it's amazing how their energy shifts. Their new names are exciting, they are actually speaking themselves as Spirit and as abundance and there is freedom and joy in that.

SpiritAbundanceMe

Although not often spoken out loud many of us have attached names to ourself like, lazy, shy, chubby, etc., as if there is no separation, you are that. This is an opportunity to create something new, something that empowers you.

I first started saying SpiritAbundanceTerces, after a while I tried a few other names, then one day while driving back from Satsang I heard in my head, OneLove and I immediately identified with it.

"OneLoveTerces, that's me," I said. So I encourage you to try a few names, practice saying who you are as Spirit and as Abundance; you'll discover what "fits" you best.

Look in the glossaries on page # 79 and choose a Spirit word and an abundance word that speaks to you. Choose two words you can own and associate with your Self and create a new "Spiritized" name for yourself. Here are some examples:

WholenessAboundingHeather

(Spirit word + abundance word + your name)

OneLoveTerces
ManaLuciousJane
GoddessGoldenJulia
MotherFertileMegan
HolyOpulentFrank
InfiniteThanksgivingDan
SpiritAbundanceMatthew

With your new name, (remember you aren't stuck with this name, you can change as often as you like) with your true name, with the name that has you be present to yourself as Spirit say the following sentence 3 times out loud.

"*My awareness of*

_____

(your Spirit word + your abundance word + Me) *as my supply is my supply.*"

Check in. Does the preceding exercise seem like "gobble-de-gook?" If we taught you how to say, "Flax flowers are blue" in

Lithuanian (Lino zydi melanai) it would sound odd too. But after a while, after we taught you more words and we practiced, you would start to be attuned to the words.

Remember the language of abundance is a foreign language.

A woman said to me, "This is like affirmations, affirmations don't work." I asked her, "Are you a mom?" She nodded, yes. Then I asked, "How often do you tell yourself you could be a better parent?" She said, "Oh, all the time." "Does saying that about yourself work?" I asked. "Are you not creating the experience of inadequacy every time you say that?" She understood.

Remember we are always affirming some view of life. What we affirm we become. Your ego will only tell you affirmations don't work when you are asserting your magnificence. Notice ego doesn't step in to contradict the power of affir-mations when you are declaring how inadequate you are.

The language of abundance takes practice because we are so conditioned to identify with a personality and a body. Our inherited language keeps separation and scarcity in place. Listen to how we speak: "*My house, your salary, Iraq's oil, the Third world, single parent, richest person, the I.R.S., etc.*"

Our language fortifies our experience of separation. We are inviting you to dwell in the language of abundance and Oneness, to embrace it with the innocence of a child and experiment with it as simply an inquiry into being present in a new way. See what shows up!

Glossary of Spirit Words

Spirit: The Whole of Life expressing as ONE body, ONE consciousness.

Absolute	Magical
All That Is	Mana
Almighty	MotherNature
Atman	Savior
Being	Self
Brahman	Spirit
Buddha nature	Universe
Chi	Universal
Christ	Wholeness
Creator	Yahweh
Deity	
Divine	Etc…
Energy	
Essence	
Eternal	
Father	
Gaia	
God	
Goddess	
Holy	
Infinite	
Lakshmi	
Light	
Lord	
Love	

Glossary of Abundance Words

Abundance: The assurance "knowingness" of the unceasing flow of supply.

Abounding	Measureless
Abundant	Millions
Affluent	Multitude
Bounteous	Munificent
Bountiful	Opulent
Burgeoning	Overflowing
Copious	Plentiful
Creamy	Prolific
Effulgent	Prosperity
Eternal	Rich
Expansive	Teeming
Fecund	Thanksgiving
Fertile	Thriving
Filled	Treasure
Flourishing	Umpteen
Fruitful	Universal
Gigantic	Unlimited
Golden	Wealthy
Gorged	
Grand	Etc.
Heaps	
Infinite	
Lavish	
Luscious	
Luxurious	
Magnificent	

"By letting go it all gets done.

The world is won by those who let it go.

But when you try and try.

The world is beyond winning."

Lao Tzu

"He who sees his lord Within every creature, Deathlessly dwelling Amidst the mortal: That man sees clearly."

Bhagavad-Gita

"The present moment is inevitable."

Shree Shree Ravi Shankar

We enter and leave this world with love in mind; in between we get distracted. In all the interviews of dying people that I've read, not one person has wished he had worked harder or acquired more. If he has a regret, it was that he had not sooner realized the charm of living in the present moment. Facing its end, the ego surrenders its arrogance and the Eternal Present emerges.

One day I was sitting with my Father just before he died and I noticed he was just staring up at the ceiling. Here was a man who had been so active, so brave, so fair all his life. My Father was an amazing human being. I wondered what he was thinking while he lay so still and quiet. I asked him, "Daddy what are you thinking about?" He looked over at me and softly said, "Love."

Life is a series of deaths-ego deaths: divorce, illness, bankruptcy, loss of job, loss of any kind. There are many ways to "die". Our egos will scamper around and strategize in order to supposedly ease the pain

and bolster our comfort but ultimately Spirit will illuminate where ever we are attached. By these "deaths" Spirit reveals to us what we are loving more than Spirit and what we are honoring more than our true Self, so that we can shift our attention back to Wholeness.

The night I finally recognized that my marriage of 22 years was over, I had an ego-death. I was so attached to being "spiritual", being the "better than thou successful" guy with **the** relationship. Now I had to face failure and my con game was up. SpiritMe showed me the loneliness of always "looking good".

I spent a night writhing in physical pain, sobbing and screaming, "You broke my heart, you broke my heart".

In the midst of this cathartic episode I became aware of a wonderful presence, of a compassionate observer who was watching **my** experience. Something other than my personality was there, being with me. At that moment I experienced my humanity I'd been running from. For a brief instant I knew how it was for all the abandoned beings sleeping in the streets and locked away in mental institutions. My pain joined me to all the forsaken and I knew we are never really alone.

Who or what is having our life experience? What a great inquiry! Since our first breath, emotions, cravings, experiences, and thoughts have been flowing through us. Our bodies and minds are always in a state of flux. But who's been there all along? Are we that stream of consciousness or are we what is watching the stream? Who is the "I" that has witnessed the passing from child to adolescent to adult? Notice all along the way we've told ourselves, " I am_____." (Fill in the blank.) What we've added to the "I am" changes, "I am sad" (happy, a man, a student, old, poor, fat) but the "I am" never changes. I request you take a few moments, close your eyes and be present to the watcher. Notice the "I am" that is there. Who is witnessing your thoughts? Who is holding the space, the vigil, for you -your personality- to have this experience? See if there isn't a watcher watching you have your life experience... That is SpiritYou. You are that. This is what Christ is talking about in John 8:58 when he says, "Before Abraham was, I am." The same "I am," the same Eternal Presence is being all of us, one presence as myriad of forms. The same eternal "I am" is being George Bush and is being the aging prostitute living in a slum in Manila. One eternal presence, one compassionate father\mother is honoring our journey, and is always inviting us home.

So when we love someone or something we really are adoring our Self, recognizing our Self over there. There are no strangers just One Presence compassionately witnessing our and its own awakening in and as all of us. Saints and mystics have always said, "We are One."

"At that day you will know that I am in the father and you in me and I in you."

John 14:20

The Abounding River journey is concerned with aligning our lives with that Eternal Presence, living the Oneness. We practice noticing where our attention is. We train ourselves to worship SpiritUs in our thinking, speaking, believing, acting and attituding.

What if all there is to notice is that you, me, God, All of life, are whole and complete, now? What if all God asks of ItSelf (that would be us) is to recognize ItSelf (that would be us)? Life is remembering. There is nothing else going on. ***It's so simple we miss it.*** The ego wants it to be a complicated and difficult journey.

On the *Abounding River* we have created money and the daily necessities of life as a sacrament to presence the fullness and fulfillment of the Eternal Present.

When you make your life about aligning yourself with Source, you can only experience having more but the increased supply is a side effect of the only game there is. Try it on, like a jacket and see if it fits.

Maybe life really is this simple. Life could be a moment-to-moment opportunity to recognize your Self, to presence how full life is *now* and to graciously receive and be grateful for all life's gifts and to recognize your Self, to presence how full life is *now* and to graciously receive and be grateful for…

The Abounding River Board Game is available online at www.withthecurrent.com

This workbook is a structure to practice remembering how magnificent, plentiful, whole and complete life is now. We are asking you to consider that unless you are being conscious, really choosing that your life is great right now, you will default to the your inner most practiced programs or ways of being. Look and see for a moment. Think about doing something totally new, or imagine you are about to broach a sensitive issue with someone you care for, or see yourself in the presence of an angry person. Can you see that you usually experience the same seemingly automatic responses? Perhaps when we are reacting to life we just defaulting to our biggest most familiar files, or ways of being, that had us survive in the past. This workbook will begin to build your muscle in being more conscious; being awake, choosing who you are being moment after moment. It will build new and rich files so that even when you forget you are the master of your experience, you might find yourself splashing in the Abounding River .

I have been practicing this for years:

I know I am perfect
Spirit
I know I am
Divine
I know I am whole
and complete unto
myself
So I choose
to be love and
give, give, give....

I've been thinking it, speaking it, believing it, attituding it and acting it out. It now occupies a space in my consciousness.

I now habitually fall into "I am Perfect Spirit" as well as " I should be doing...." I am making Divine Love a habit. I call it *Spiritizing*, aligning my being with my highest notion of myself as God.

"Carpenters bend wood; fletchers bend arrows; wise men fashion themselves."
Gautama Buddha

"Perception is a learned phenomenon."
Deepak Chopra

I had some pretty strong files of being inadequate, and would often resort to them, no matter what my outer accomplishments might look like. However now, after really embracing this practice and confronting the power of those demeaning messages I told myself, I not only appreciate who I am, I love myself.

"As a single footstep will not make a path on the earth, so a single thought will not make a pathway in the mind. To make a deep physical path, we walk again and again. To make a deep mental path, we must think over and over the kind of thoughts we wish to dominate our lives."
Henry D. Thoreau

This is a forty-two day workbook, a forty-two day experiment in giving your attention over to how full life is now, how great you are now. This is a tool to break the gravitational pull of the scarcity matrix and awaken to the Abundance that is always eternally present. Play with this practice for the sake of play, expectations suck the fun out of life anyway.

If you ever find yourself wondering whether "it's" working, and you probably will, simply look at all you have to be grateful for. Surrender to all you are blessed with and be astonished by all that is given. The prize is your consciousness being aware it Self.

Your ego isn't going to like this practice, it will make the practice wrong and stupid and make you silly for taking the time to practice. After all, your ego has more important things to pay attention too, important goals to accomplish, and bills to pay.

Your habitual nature will attempt to convince you to stop practicing because "it"

isn't going to work, notice how your ego is not interested in the now, and then when you miss a few days of practice your ego will then make you wrong for not having the discipline to practice. Your ego has no interest in you experiencing your self as whole, as God. Every moment you get to choose what master you serve, to what you devote your consciousness. We worship what we give our attention to. This is a prayer book.

Instructions

> "The mind turned outward results in thoughts and objects. Turned inwards it becomes itself the Self."
> *Ramana Maharshi*

Listening to Spirit

This practice is by no means complete. The *Abounding River* is an exercise in being conscious in thought, speech, belief, action, and attitude. This book dwells in the world of thought, action and language. We are not exploring the aspect of ourselves that is subtler than thought.

On the *Abounding River* we are not attempting to quiet our thoughts, we are holding the Divine in them.

We recommend a daily meditation practice, a daily dip in the sublime silence of our Self, as another way to awaken to our Divine Nature.

Meditation is a powerful tool to lessen the grip of the habitual nature of the ego and experience the presence of the your eternal presence.

There are a lot of ways to meditate, to listen to Spirit. If you don't have a practice we suggest the following:

Sit comfortably in a quiet place with an erect spine. Remind yourself there is nowhere to get to, there is only this moment. Close your eyes, breath through your nose and follow your breath. Inhale-exhale. When you notice your mind wandering, as it will, simply and effortlessly shift your attention back to your breath. Follow your breath in (receive it) and out (release it) with an attitude of no expectation.

In meditation have your attitude be "so what." Gently bring your attention back to your breath when you notice it elsewhere.

Practice 20 minutes everyday as a devotion to God and a gift to yourself.

Everyday in the workbook we remind you to practice listening to Spirit and have created a space for you to write down anything you might hear or any insights you might have. You might ask your Self, "What would God or Spirit do now?" "If the Whole of life were speaking to me, what would It say?"

In the *Resources* section we have included other recommendations for meditation practices.

Speaking and Listening as Spirit

Before beginning, share with your partner anything that you might be thinking or concerned about that would inhibit you openly practicing being the *current* or quality of Spirit, you are working on that day; being *Responsible, Worthy, Loving Accepting, Grateful, Generous,* or *Abundant*.

Have your partner share with you. Simply listen to one another. There is nothing to fix or change, just be with one another.

Pick who is partner A and who is partner B.

Partner A begins (using their *Spirit* and *Abundance* words when called for).

Partner B responds using partner A's *Spirit* and *Abundance* words when called for.

Repeat this 11 times.

Then Partner A switch with Partner B so that the focus of the exercise is reversed and repeat entire exercise. You will now be using Partner B's *Spirit* and *Abundance* words when called for. There will be 44 repetitions in all.

"The real purpose of the world is to use it to correct your unbelief."
A Course In Miracles

We are always affirming something. This is an opportunity to practice speaking and listening as the Spirit being you are. The only thing in the way are those practiced habitual ways of being.

Notice the emotional charge on those really deep habits, the bigger the charge the more "real" they occur, the more apt we are to get hooked in that program. Bring some emotion to these new files you are building. Be excited, enthusiastic, be moved by yourself and that you are freeing yourself from the scarcity matrix. Be proud of your devotion to God as your consciousness. Charge this partner work with emotional energy.

Acknowledgement\ Exploration Question

"The outer situation is always a reflection of the collective inner situation."

Peace Pilgrim

Each day this is an opportunity to explore your "view of life." to experience any constraints that "view" has and perhaps to start investing more of your attention in being a quality of Spirit.

This is an opportunity to say what you don't want to say and be honest with yourself and others. This part of the practice makes a big difference in freeing yourself of your P.racticed A.part S.carcity T.ale.

Being Generous

"He who does not know about service knows even less about Mastership." *Tirmizi*

Everyday there is an opportunity to Be Generous. We suggest you go out of your way and really S-T-R-E-T-C-H beyond where you are comfortable, i.e. pay the toll for the car behind you, feed a stranger, buy flowers for an acquaintance, clean someone's house, watch someone's children.

Give in a way that expands your sense of yourSelf, especially when you think you have little or nothing to give. Remember this is about being in the flow.

Laughter!!!!

"The greatest prayer you could ever pray would be to laugh everyday. For when you do, it elevates the vibratory frequency within your being such that you could heal your whole body." *Ramtha*

Laugh out loud 1 minute everyday. There is no reason to laugh, you simply laugh for the sake of laughing. This is an exercise in being insignificant, watch your ego's resistance. This is a practice in mastery because you are generating your being without any "outer" cause or condition. Laughing opens up the physiology to the presence of health and abundance.

Being Grateful

Everyday there is a reminder to Be Grateful (Great-Full). Gratitude and inadequacy can't occupy the same moment.

At meals look and see all there is to be grateful for-remember the tuna fish sandwich. Take notice of all the beings that participate in the food you eat. Count them all with gratitude; and note how the whole of life is working for your existence.

The farmers, truck drivers, fisherman, engineers, shop-keepers, bakers, earth-worms, rain... all of them are in the body of your life supporting you.

Each time you exchange money or pay bills gratefully participate with Spirit as the phone company, the government, the clerk. Be moved by our interdependence and be grateful for the Whole body of life. At the end of the day if you find you have forgotten to be grateful, just review the day and give thanks for all you received. It is never to late to be grateful.

"When you drink from the stream, remember the source."
Chinese proverb

"The Divine wants to be fully expressed and experienced as you. Be moved by your devotion to God as your consciousness."
Matthew Engelhart

Mirror Work

On Worth current days there is an opportunity to practice mirror work. This is really about being sure the person in the mirror owns what you are saying, that what you are saying is land-ing over there with you, the person in the mirror.

This is an opportunity to relish yourself as a Divine creation. Shower the regard on yourself that you usu-ally reserve for small chil-dren, animals, and your most intimate relations. How could you possibly experience abundance at a Divine level if you can't embrace God as you?

I promise you miracles out of practicing being with the person in the mirror. Let all your criticisms go, simply don't give in or get stopped by them. Stay with the person in the mirror keep your attention on being with him or her.

Writing Before Bed

" The constant dripping of water wears away the stone."
Sufi saying

There is nothing sexy about this part of the practice. Writing before bed is making a new groove in your aware-ness using the physical act of writing – it is programming abundance and Oneness into your consciousness. Notice your resistance and don't get stopped by it. This is a pow-erful part of the pracitice.

Notes / Journal

"What we are looking for is what is looking."
St. Francis of Assisi

This is your section to write whatever you want to remember or note about your practice. You may

have insights to get in touch with people, apologize, acknowledge, express thanks, etc. You might jot down inspirations or ideas or actions to take.

Resources

The Abounding River Game is a board game designed to practice the being of abundance. Playing the game is an opportunity to put your attention on the six currents and presence how blessed we are with friends, family and community. Available online at www.withthecurrent.com

Café Gratitude is a living foods cafe in California and is a live version of the **Abounding River Board Game**. Delicious and healthy foods are served in an atmosphere of thanksgiving. The staff aspires to be present to life's fullness and will invite you to play in a world of plenty. As of this publication date there are four **Café Gratitude** locations, two in San Francisco, one in Berkeley and one in San Rafael. For more information call 415-824-4652 or visit www.cafegratitude.com.

The Abounding River Workshop is an intensive training in the being of abundance. It is offered in both a one and two day format for groups and individuals. Please visit www.withthecurrent.com for a schedule of upcoming workshops or for information on how to host a workshop in your area.

Art of Living Foundation Meditation (Sahaj Samadi) and purifying breath work (Sadarshan Kriya) taught under the auspices of living master Sri Sri Ravi Shankar. Visit www.artofliving.com

The Landmark Forum Three days of powerful transformation in the venue of a Socratic inquiry. www.landmarkeducation.com

Book Credits

Art Direction, Book Design and Backgrounds by **Julia D. Stege** of **Graphic Girlz** in Sonoma County, California. Visit www.GraphicGirlz.com.

Original Illustrations by **Frank Riccio** of Charlottesville, Virginia.

Production by **Dan Yokum** of **Yokum Designs** in Ithaca, New York. Visit www.YokumDesigns.com

Printing Services by **Robert Clark** of **Norcal Printing** in San Francisco, California. Contact: rmcs@aol.com.

Special Thanks!

To Michael, Carl, Jan, Julia, Frank and Dan!

DAY ONE

"The currents of Universal Being circulate through me; I am part and parcel of God."
Ralph Waldo Emerson

EXPLORATION

What is an inherited belief you have about money that inhibits your experience of abundance? What is something you would like to believe about money that would have you aware of abundance? Share both these beliefs with someone in your life.

River Guide- You are the source of your beliefs. Empower ones that empower you.

LISTEN TO SPIRIT

_____
_____
_____
_____
_____

BEING GENEROUS

Give some form of supply (money, food, clothes, time, etc.) to someone remembering money or supply doesn't go anywhere and releasing-receiving are ONE and the same.

Log Here

_____
_____

BEING GRATEFUL

Did I acknowledge and thank _____ Me as the
(Spirit word)   (Abundance word)

money, credit cards, plants, fishermen, shopkeepers, cooks, natural gas, truck drivers, etc. for participating in every meal and every product I used today?
Today I am especially acknowledging farmers!

LISTENING AND SPEAKING AS SPIRIT

Partner A says
I am responsible for my thoughts, speech, beliefs, actions and attitudes, which create my experience of life. I am the creator of my experience. I choose to be _____ now!
(Abundance word)

Partner B responds
_____ , you are the creator of
(Partner's name)

your experience of life. You now choose to be _____ .
(Abundance word)

Repeat 11x

Partner B says
You are responsible for your thoughts, speech, beliefs, actions and attitudes, which create your experience of life. You are the creator of your experience. You choose to be _____ now.
(Abundance word)

Partner A responds
I, _____ am the creator of my
(Your name)

experience of life. I now choose to be
_____ .
(Abundance word)

Repeat 11x

Now Partner A switch with Partner B so that the focus of the exercise is reversed.

Repeat exercise.

LAUGHTER!

☐ I laughed out loud for one minute today!

BEFORE BED
(write 11 times)
I now take responsibility for being the creator of my experience. I am present to my _____ now.
(Abundance word)

NOTES/LOG
_____
_____
_____
_____
_____
_____
_____
_____
_____
_____
_____
_____

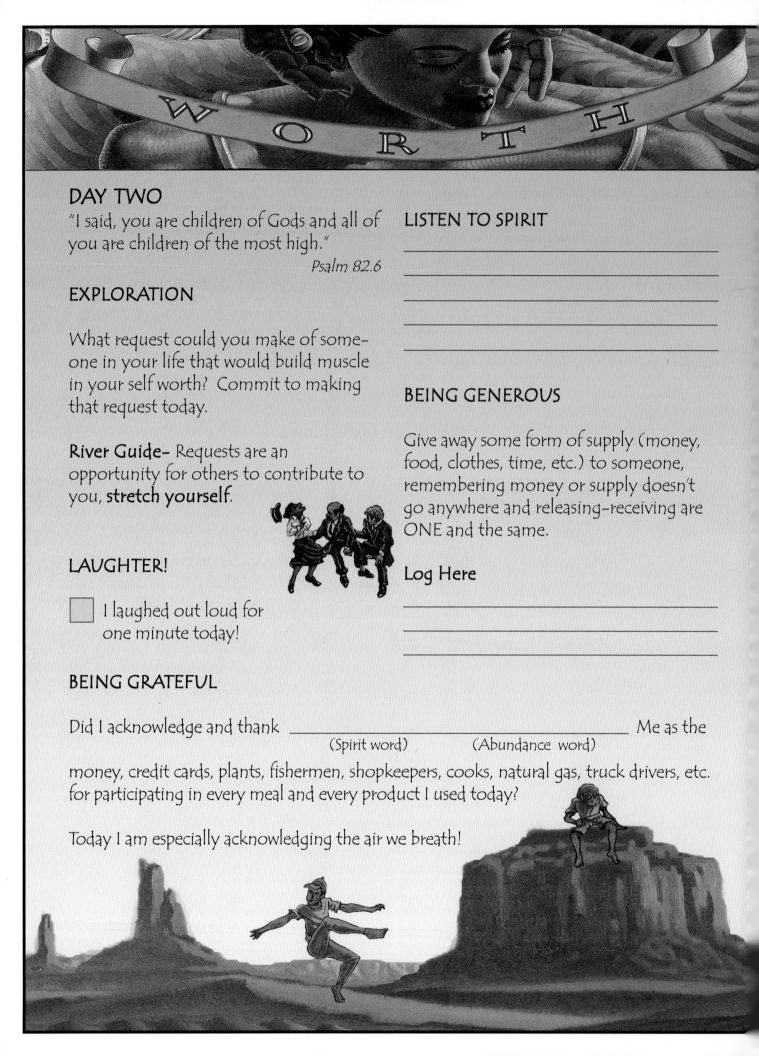

DAY TWO

"I said, you are children of Gods and all of you are children of the most high."

Psalm 82.6

EXPLORATION

What request could you make of someone in your life that would build muscle in your self worth? Commit to making that request today.

River Guide- Requests are an opportunity for others to contribute to you, **stretch yourself**.

LAUGHTER!

☐ I laughed out loud for one minute today!

BEING GRATEFUL

LISTEN TO SPIRIT

_____

_____

_____

_____

_____

BEING GENEROUS

Give away some form of supply (money, food, clothes, time, etc.) to someone, remembering money or supply doesn't go anywhere and releasing-receiving are ONE and the same.

Log Here

_____

_____

_____

Did I acknowledge and thank _____ Me as the
                              (Spirit word)   (Abundance word)

money, credit cards, plants, fishermen, shopkeepers, cooks, natural gas, truck drivers, etc. for participating in every meal and every product I used today?

Today I am especially acknowledging the air we breath!

LISTENING AND SPEAKING AS SPIRIT

Partner A (says to Partner B)

_____ is having a
(Spirit word)

_____ experience. I am
(your name)

perfect _____ . I love
(Spirit word)

_____ as my life and as all of
(Spirit word)

life. I am worthy of everything
wonderful, all the _____
_____ Me is. (Abundance word)
(Spirit word)

Partner B (responds)

You are _____ expressed as
(Spirit word)

_____ . You celebrate
(Partner A's name)

your _____ worth now.
(Spirit word)

Repeat 11x

NOTES/LOG

_____
_____
_____
_____
_____
_____
_____
_____
_____
_____

Partner B

_____ is having a _____
(Spirit word)   (Partner A's name)

experience. You are perfect _____
(Spirit word)

You love _____ You as your life
(Spirit word)

and as all of life. You are worthy of
everything wonderful, all the

_____ _____ You is.
(Abundance word) (Spirit word)

Partner A responds:
I am _____ expressed as _____
(Spirit word)   (Your name)

I celebrate my _____ worth now.
(Spirit word)

Repeat 11 X

Now Partner A switch with Partner B
so that the focus of the exercise is
reversed.

Repeat exercise.

BEFORE BED
(say 11 times to the person in the mirror)
I am worthy of everything wonderful.
I am _____ expressed as me.
(Spirit word)

I love being

_____ Me.
(Spirit word)   (Abundance word)

DAY THREE

L O V E • A C C E P T A N C E

"Love thy neighbor as thy self."

Matthew 19:19

EXPLORATION

What do you say isn't the best about your life? Who creates it as the best or not?

River Guide- Who would you have to be to create everything, every moment as the best?

LAUGHTER! ☐

I laughed out loud for one minute today!

BEING GRATEFUL

Did I acknowledge and thank _____ Me as the

(Spirit word)   (Abundance word)

money, credit cards, plants, fishermen, shopkeepers, cooks, natural gas, truck drivers, etc. for participating in every meal and every product I used today?

Today I am especially acknowledging-fresh water.

LISTEN TO SPIRIT

_____
_____
_____
_____
_____

BEING GENEROUS

Give away some form of supply (money, food, clothes, time, etc.) to someone, remembering money or supply doesn't go anywhere and releasing-receiving are ONE and the same.

Log Here

_____
_____
_____
_____

SPEAKING AND LISTENING AS SPIRIT

Partner A says

I trust _____ completely. I surrender
     (Spirit word)

all concerns to _____ knowing
       (Spirit word)

_____ is being only the best as my
(Spirit word)

life now!

Partner B responds

You trust _____ as your life now
      (Spirit word)

knowing _____ is always being the
     (Spirit word)

best for all of life.

Repeat 11 times

Partner B says

You trust _____ completely. You
      (Spirit word)

surrender all concerns to _____
         (Spirit word)

knowing _____ is being the best as
     (Spirit word)

my life now!

Partner A responds

I trust _____ as my life now knowing
     (Spirit word)

_____ is always the best for all of life.
(Spirit word)

Repeat 11 times

Now Partner A switch with Partner B
so that the focus of the exercise is reversed.

Repeat exercise

BEFORE BED

Look in the mirror and be loving. Hug
yourself. Say, "I adore you, I relish and
revere myself. I am _____ 's
      (Spirit word)

perfect expression." Keep repeating this.
Blow a kiss to yourself. Wrap your arms
around your self. Practice being
_____ You, loving
(Spirit word)

_____ You for 2 mushy minutes!
(Spirit word)

NOTES/LOG

_____
_____
_____
_____
_____
_____
_____

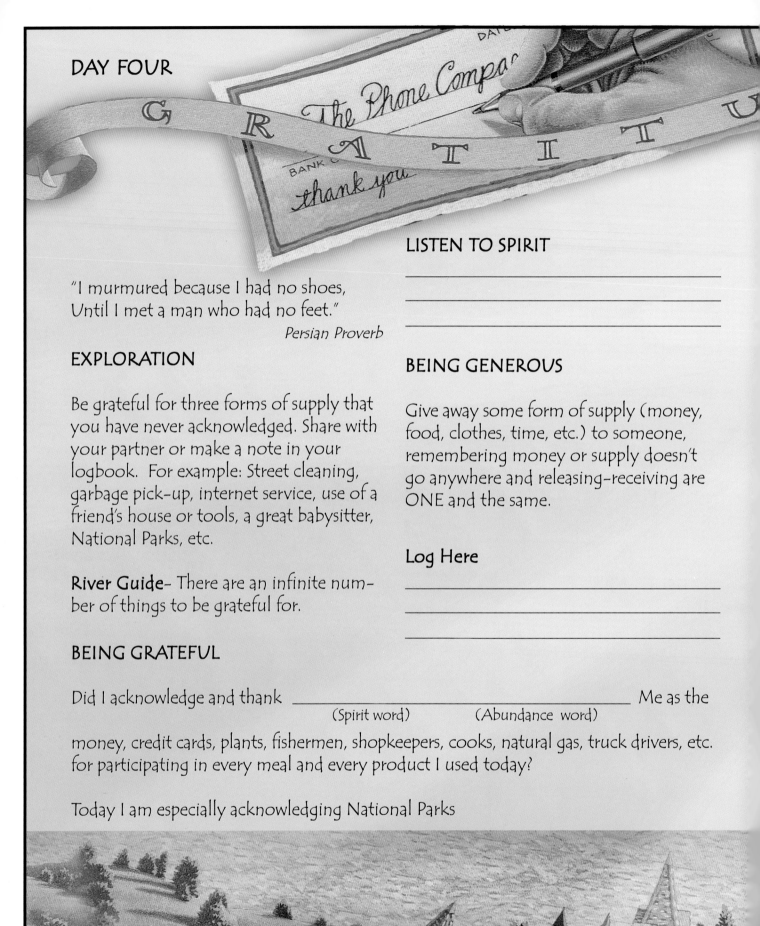

DAY FOUR

"I murmured because I had no shoes,
Until I met a man who had no feet."
Persian Proverb

EXPLORATION

Be grateful for three forms of supply that you have never acknowledged. Share with your partner or make a note in your logbook. For example: Street cleaning, garbage pick-up, internet service, use of a friend's house or tools, a great babysitter, National Parks, etc.

River Guide- There are an infinite number of things to be grateful for.

BEING GRATEFUL

LISTEN TO SPIRIT

_____
_____
_____

BEING GENEROUS

Give away some form of supply (money, food, clothes, time, etc.) to someone, remembering money or supply doesn't go anywhere and releasing-receiving are ONE and the same.

Log Here

_____
_____
_____

Did I acknowledge and thank _____ Me as the
                              (Spirit word)   (Abundance word)

money, credit cards, plants, fishermen, shopkeepers, cooks, natural gas, truck drivers, etc. for participating in every meal and every product I used today?

Today I am especially acknowledging National Parks

SPEAKING AND LISTENING AS SPIRIT

Partner A says

I am grateful for all of life. I am being thankful for everything I see and everything I don't see.

Partner B responds

You are the thankfulness of_____.
(Spirit word)

Repeat 11 times

Partner B says

You are grateful for all of life. You are being thankful for everything you see and everything you don't see.

Partner A responds:

I am the thankfulness of _____.
(Spirit word)

Repeat 11 times

Now Partner A switch with Partner B so that the focus of the exercise is reversed.

Repeat exercise

NOTES/LOG

_____
_____
_____
_____
_____
_____
_____

☐ LAUGHTER!

I laughed out loud for one minute today!

BEFORE BED

Sit still, close your eyes and imagine sitting at the side of a gushing spring. For as long as anyone can remember this spring has been overflowing with clean, fresh, delicious water for all to enjoy. Be grateful for the benevolence of the earth. Put your attention on all that has been given to you. For five minutes think of all you have to be grateful for.

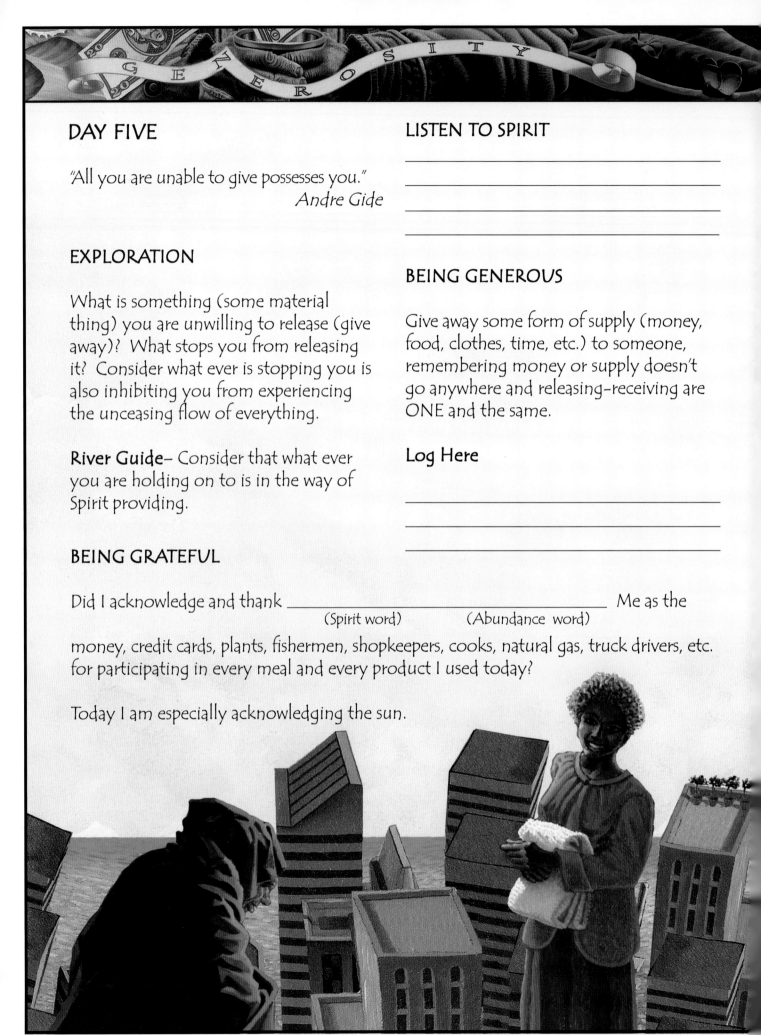

DAY FIVE

"All you are unable to give possesses you."
Andre Gide

EXPLORATION

What is something (some material thing) you are unwilling to release (give away)? What stops you from releasing it? Consider what ever is stopping you is also inhibiting you from experiencing the unceasing flow of everything.

River Guide– Consider that what ever you are holding on to is in the way of Spirit providing.

BEING GRATEFUL

Did I acknowledge and thank _____ Me as the
　　　　　　　　　　　　　　　　(Spirit word)　　　　(Abundance word)

money, credit cards, plants, fishermen, shopkeepers, cooks, natural gas, truck drivers, etc. for participating in every meal and every product I used today?

Today I am especially acknowledging the sun.

LISTEN TO SPIRIT

_____
_____
_____
_____

BEING GENEROUS

Give away some form of supply (money, food, clothes, time, etc.) to someone, remembering money or supply doesn't go anywhere and releasing-receiving are ONE and the same.

Log Here

_____
_____
_____

SPEAKING AND LISTENING AS SPIRIT

Partner A says:
As I serve others, I serve myself.
As I serve myself, all are served. I
am completely fulfilled giving to the
entire body of _____ Me.
(Spirit word)

Partner B responds:
You relish contributing to everyone
as the whole of yourself.

Repeat 11 times

Partner B says:
As you serve others, you serve yourself
As you serve yourself, all are served.
You are completely fulfilled giving to the
entire body of_____ You.
(Spirit word)

Partner A responds:
I relish contributing to everyone as the
whole of myself.

Repeat 11 times

Now Partner A switch with Partner B so
that the focus of the exercise is reversed.

Repeat exercise

BEFORE BED

Sit quietly and close your eyes. Keep your
awareness on your breath. Notice your
inhale (receive) and exhale
(release). Be present to all the supply you
receive on the inhale and all that you
release on the exhale. Be grateful for the
constant flow of supply that moves
through you. Be present to
releasing and receiving.

☐ LAUGHTER!

I laughed out loud for
one minute today!

NOTES/LOG

_____
_____
_____
_____
_____
_____
_____
_____
_____

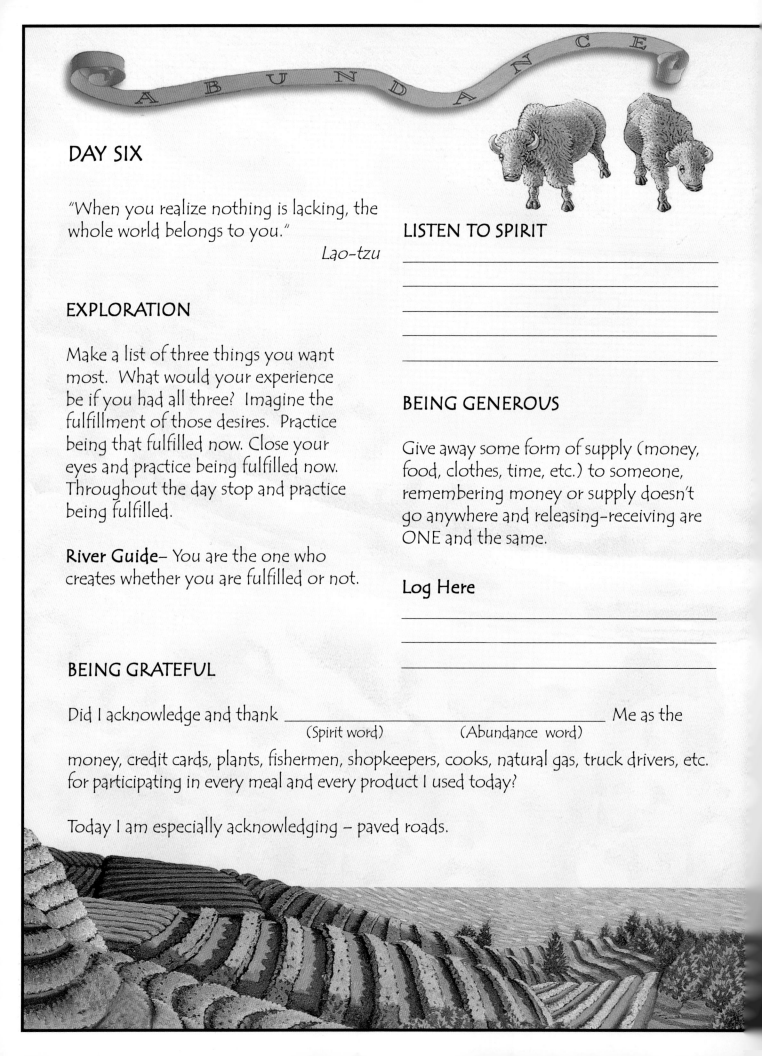

DAY SIX

"When you realize nothing is lacking, the whole world belongs to you."

Lao-tzu

EXPLORATION

Make a list of three things you want most. What would your experience be if you had all three? Imagine the fulfillment of those desires. Practice being that fulfilled now. Close your eyes and practice being fulfilled now. Throughout the day stop and practice being fulfilled.

River Guide– You are the one who creates whether you are fulfilled or not.

LISTEN TO SPIRIT

_____
_____
_____
_____
_____

BEING GENEROUS

Give away some form of supply (money, food, clothes, time, etc.) to someone, remembering money or supply doesn't go anywhere and releasing-receiving are ONE and the same.

Log Here

_____
_____
_____

BEING GRATEFUL

Did I acknowledge and thank _____ Me as the
                (Spirit word)   (Abundance word)

money, credit cards, plants, fishermen, shopkeepers, cooks, natural gas, truck drivers, etc. for participating in every meal and every product I used today?

Today I am especially acknowledging – paved roads.

SPEAKING AND LISTENING AS SPIRIT

Partner A says:

My awareness of _____ Me
　　　　　　　　(Spirit word)

as my supply is my supply. I am present
to being lavishly fulfilled now.

Partner B responds:

You are aware of _____ You
　　　　　　　　(Spirit word)

as abundance. You are all that
_____ is now.
(Spirit word)

Repeat 11 times

Partner B says:

Your awareness of _____ You
　　　　　　　　(Spirit word)

as your supply is your supply. You are
present to being lavishly fulfilled now.

Partner A responds:

I am aware of _____ Me as
　　　　　　(Spirit word)

abundance. I am all that
_____ is now.
(Spirit word)

Repeat 11 times

Now Partner A switch with
Partner B so that the focus
of the exercise is reversed.

Repeat exercise

NOTES/LOG

_____

_____

_____

_____

_____

_____

_____

_____

_____

LAUGHTER!

☐ I laughed out loud for
one minute today!

BEFORE BED:

(Write 11 times)
"I am fulfilled in this now moment. I
am present to being abundance now."

DAY SEVEN

"So shall my word be that goeth forth out of my mouth: it shall not return to me void, but it shall accomplish that which I please and it shall prosper in the thing where to I sent it."

Isaiah 55:11

EXPLORATION

What is something you are not being responsible for? "It just is that way." "They are just that way." Now how can you create that same situation as an opportunity to be responsible?

River Guide– Take a moment and reflect on your life and now like a proud 4 year old say, "I'm creating it!"

BEING GRATEFUL

LISTEN TO SPIRIT

_____

_____

_____

_____

_____

BEING GENEROUS

Give some form of supply (money, food, clothes, time, etc.) to someone remembering money or supply doesn't go anywhere and releasing-receiving are ONE and the same.

Log Here

_____

_____

Did I acknowledge and thank _____ _____ Me as the
 (Spirit word)   (Abundance word)

money, credit cards, plants, fishermen, shopkeepers, cooks, natural gas, truck drivers, etc. for participating in every meal and every product I used today?

Today I am especially acknowledging flowers!

LISTENING AND SPEAKING AS SPIRIT

Partner A says:

_____ Me is everywhere and is always
(Spirit word)

present, as everything I see and don't see,
_____ Me is always, taking on shape,
(Spirit word)

form and experience as more and more of
what it is, of what I am. Abundance is
everywhere and is always present, as
_____ Me taking on shape, form and
(Spirit word)

experience now.

Partner B responds:

You _____ are _____ expressed
(Your name)   (Spirit word)

as lavish abundance now!

Repeat 11 times

Partner B says:

_____You is everywhere and is always
(Spirit word)

present, as everything you see and don't see.
_____You is always taking on shape,
(Spirit word)

form and experience as more and more of
what it is, of what you are. Abundance is
everywhere and is always present as
_____ You taking on shape, form and
(Spirit word)

experience now.

Partner A responds:

I _____ am _____ expressed as
(Your name)   (Spirit word)

lavish abundance now!

Repeat 11 times

Now Partner A switch with Partner B
so that the focus of the exercise is
reversed. *Repeat exercise*

LAUGHTER!

☐ I laughed out loud for
one minute today!

BEFORE BED
(write 11 times)

I am the creator of my experience.
Where I put my attention is the source of
my experience. I love thinking, speaking,
believing, acting and attituding as
_____ Me now.
(Spirit word)   (Abundance word)

NOTES/LOG

_____
_____
_____
_____
_____
_____
_____
_____
_____
_____
_____
_____

DAY EIGHT

"If God had wanted me otherwise He would have created me otherwise."
                                    Johann von Goethe

EXPLORATION

Acknowledge five things you love about your self.

River Guide– Why not love yourself as God's creation?

LAUGHTER!

☐ I laughed out loud for one minute today!

LISTEN TO SPIRIT

_____
_____
_____
_____
_____

BEING GENEROUS

Give away some form of supply (money, food, clothes, time, etc.) to someone, remembering money or supply doesn't go anywhere and releasing-receiving are ONE and the same.

Log Here

_____
_____
_____

BEING GRATEFUL

Did I acknowledge and thank _____ Me as the
                                    (Spirit word)   (Abundance word)

money, credit cards, plants, fishermen, shopkeepers, cooks, natural gas, truck drivers, etc. for participating in every meal and every product I used today?

Today I am especially acknowledging trees.

LISTENING AND SPEAKING AS SPIRIT

Partner A:

I am perfect _____ expressing as
 (Spirit word)

_____ . I am worthy of everything
 (your name)

wonderful. I love and adore myself as a
Divine creation.

Partner B:

You are a Divine creation. You are love
expressed as _____ .
 (your name)

Repeat 11 times

NOTES/LOG

_____

_____

_____

_____

_____

Partner B says:

You are perfect _____ expressing
 (Spirit word)

as_____ . You are worthy of
 (your name)

everything wonderful. You love and
adore yourself as a Divine
creation.

Partner A responds:

I am a Divine creation. I am love
expressed as _____ .
 (Your name)

Repeat 11 times

Now Partner A switch with Partner B
so that the focus of the exercise is
reversed.

Repeat exercise

BEFORE BED
(say 11 times to the person in the mirror)

I adore _____ as the whole of life and I adore _____ as me. I am
 (Spirit word)   (Spirit word)

_____ loving having a_____ experience. I am worthy of everything
 (Spirit word)   (Your name)

and anything whole _____ Me is.
 (Spirit word)

DAY NINE

LOVE • ACCEPTANCE

"Resistance causes pain and lethargy. It is when we practice acceptance that new possibilities appear."

Anonymous

EXPLORATION

Acknowledge two events in life that you don't trust as _____'s
(Spirit word)

perfect expression. Identify what it would take for you to bring love and acceptance to those events. Share that with your partner.

River Guide– Who are you to judge Spirit? What part of Spirit expressing don't you love and accept?

☐ LAUGHTER!
I laughed out loud for one minute today!

LISTEN TO SPIRIT

_____
_____
_____
_____
_____

BEING GENEROUS

Give away some form of supply (money, food, clothes, time, etc.) to someone, remembering money or supply doesn't go anywhere and releasing-receiving are ONE and the same.

Log Here

_____
_____
_____
_____

BEING GRATEFUL

Did I acknowledge and thank _____ Me as the
(Spirit word)   (Abundance word)

money, credit cards, plants, fishermen, shopkeepers, cooks, natural gas, truck drivers, etc. for participating in every meal and every product I used today?

Today I am being especially grateful for the ocean.

SPEAKING AND LISTENING AS SPIRIT

Partner A says:

I know_____ is working through
　　　　(Spirit word)

me and through all of life for everyone's
best now. I trust today's events as

_____ 's love expressing the best
(Spirit word)

for all of life now.

Partner B responds:

You trust your life and all of life as

_____ 's perfect expression now.
(Spirit word)

Repeat 11 times

Partner B says:

You know_____ is working
　　　　(Spirit word)

through you and through
all of life for everyone's best now. You
trust today's events as _____'s
　　　　　　　　　　　　　(Spirit word)

love expressing the best for all of life now.

Partner A responds:

I trust my life and all of life as
_____ 's perfect expression now.
(Spirit word)

Repeat 11 times

Now Partner A switch with Partner B so
that the focus of the exercise is reversed.

Repeat exercise

NOTES/LOG

_____
_____
_____
_____
_____
_____
_____
_____

BEFORE BED
(Write 11 times)

_____is out picturing as my life
　　(Spirit word)

now. I see that all life is working as One
body for _____'s perfect
　　　　　　　　(Spirit word)

expression now. I am peaceful in my faith.

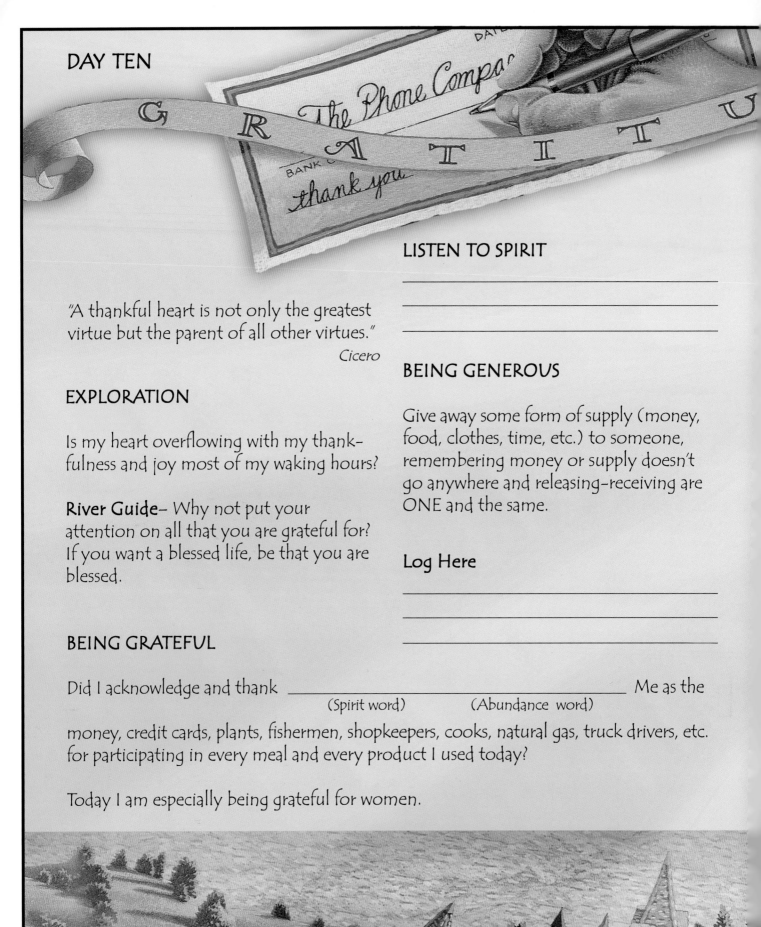

DAY TEN

"A thankful heart is not only the greatest virtue but the parent of all other virtues."

Cicero

EXPLORATION

Is my heart overflowing with my thankfulness and joy most of my waking hours?

River Guide– Why not put your attention on all that you are grateful for? If you want a blessed life, be that you are blessed.

BEING GRATEFUL

Did I acknowledge and thank _____ Me as the
(Spirit word)   (Abundance word)

money, credit cards, plants, fishermen, shopkeepers, cooks, natural gas, truck drivers, etc. for participating in every meal and every product I used today?

Today I am especially being grateful for women.

LISTEN TO SPIRIT

_____
_____
_____

BEING GENEROUS

Give away some form of supply (money, food, clothes, time, etc.) to someone, remembering money or supply doesn't go anywhere and releasing-receiving are ONE and the same.

Log Here

_____
_____
_____

SPEAKING AND LISTENING AS SPIRIT

Partner A says:
I am grateful for what I have. I am always focused in the present moment where I have everything wonderful I desire, I am filled with gratitude.

Partner B responds:
You are grateful and blessed in this now moment.

Repeat 11 times

Partner B says:
You are grateful for what you have. You are always focused in the present moment where you have everything wonderful you desire. You are filled with gratitude.

Partner A responds:
I am grateful and blessed in this now moment.

Repeat 11 times

Now Partner A switch with Partner B so that the focus of the exercise is reversed.

Repeat exercise

_____
_____
_____
_____
_____
_____
_____

☐ LAUGHTER!

I laughed out loud for one minute today!

BEFORE BED

Take one meal you ate today and make a list of all the expressions of Spirit that contributed to that meal. Let yourself be present to all the ways that the whole body of Spirit contributes to you.

DAY ELEVEN

"My religion is kindness."

Dalai Lama

EXPLORATION

Am I a joyful giver, do I share money generously with others knowing that giving and receiving are one and the same?

River Guide– Who would Spirit deny? Who are you to deny Spirit over there?

BEING GRATEFUL

Did I acknowledge and thank _____
                                        (Spirit word)

_____ Me as the money,
 (Abundance word)

credit cards, plants, fishermen, shopkeepers, cooks, natural gas, truck drivers, etc. for participating in every meal and every product I used today?

Today I am especially acknowledging eyes.

LISTEN TO SPIRIT

_____
_____
_____
_____

BEING GENEROUS

Give away some form of supply (money, food, clothes, time, etc.) to someone, remembering money or supply doesn't go anywhere and releasing-receiving are ONE and the same.

Log Here

_____
_____
_____
_____
_____
_____

SPEAKING AND LISTENING AS SPIRIT

Partner A says:
I am deeply grateful for everything I receive and I enjoy giving to others with an attitude of love and service.

Partner B responds:
You are thankful for the opportunity to share with others as
_____Wholeness You.
(Spirit word)

Repeat 11 times

Partner B says:
You are deeply grateful for everything you receive and you enjoy giving to others with an attitude of love and service.

Partner A responds:
I am thankful for the opportunity to share with others as
_____ wholeness me.
(Spirit word)

Repeat 11 times

Now Partner A switch with Partner B so that the focus of the exercise is reversed.

Repeat exercise

BEFORE BED

What would you love to contribute to another or be known for having contributed to the world? For example, sending your mother on a cruise, ending the AIDS epidemic. How could you make that contribution now? What action could you take, what form of supply could you give away? For example, put a dollar in a savings account for your mom's cruise, take a meal to an AIDS patient, etc.

◻ LAUGHTER!

I laughed out loud for one minute today!

NOTES/LOG

_____
_____
_____
_____
_____
_____
_____
_____
_____
_____

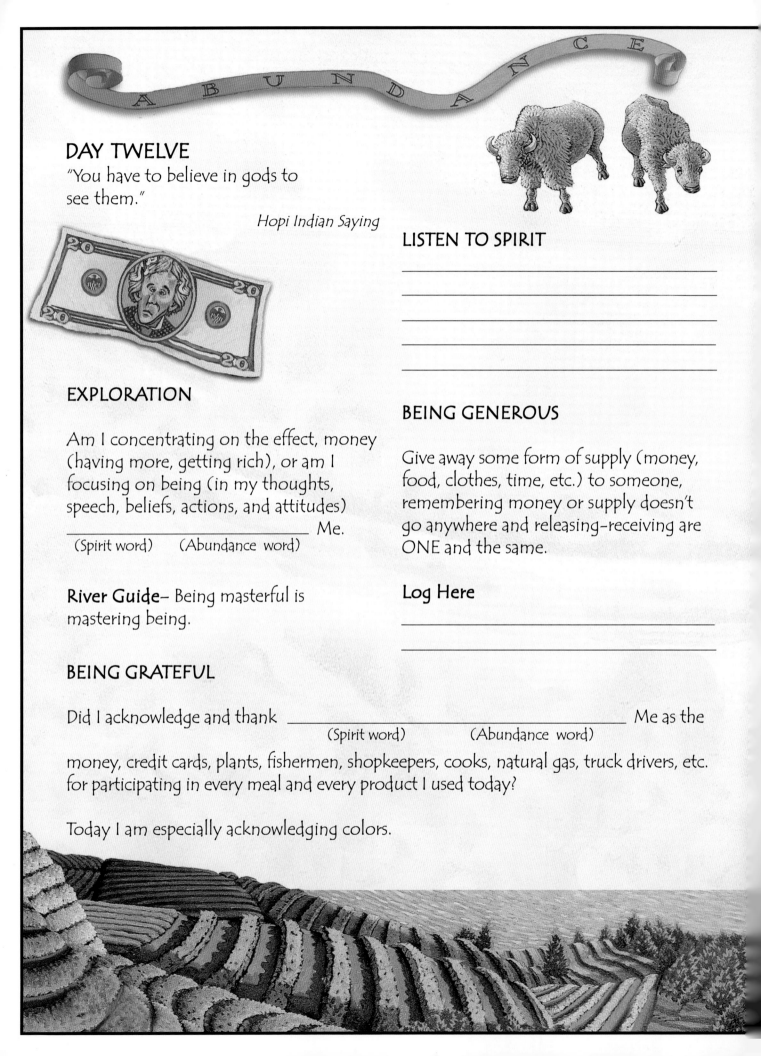

ABUNDANCE

DAY TWELVE

"You have to believe in gods to see them."

Hopi Indian Saying

LISTEN TO SPIRIT

_____

_____

_____

_____

_____

EXPLORATION

Am I concentrating on the effect, money (having more, getting rich), or am I focusing on being (in my thoughts, speech, beliefs, actions, and attitudes) _____ Me.
(Spirit word)   (Abundance word)

River Guide– Being masterful is mastering being.

BEING GENEROUS

Give away some form of supply (money, food, clothes, time, etc.) to someone, remembering money or supply doesn't go anywhere and releasing-receiving are ONE and the same.

Log Here

_____

_____

BEING GRATEFUL

Did I acknowledge and thank _____ Me as the
(Spirit word)   (Abundance word)

money, credit cards, plants, fishermen, shopkeepers, cooks, natural gas, truck drivers, etc. for participating in every meal and every product I used today?

Today I am especially acknowledging colors.

SPEAKING AND LISTENING AS SPIRIT

Partner A says:
I am abundance constantly expressing into shape, form and experience by my thoughts, speech, beliefs, actions and attitudes. My conscious awareness of this truth is unlimited so my experience of abundance is unlimited.

Partner B responds:
You _____ sculpt
(Partner's name)

_____ substance with your
(Spirit word)

thoughts, speech, beliefs, actions and attitudes as your experience of abundance now!

Repeat 11 times

Partner B says:
You are abundance constantly expressing into shape, form and experience by your thoughts, speech, beliefs, actions and attitudes. Your conscious awareness of this truth is unlimited so your experience of abundance is unlimited.

Partner A responds:
I sculpt _____ substance with
(Spirit word)

my thoughts, speech, beliefs, actions and attitudes as my experience of abundance now.

Repeat 11 times

BEFORE BED:

Sit quietly on your bed and close your eyes. Take a few deep breaths. Imagine having a pot of gold coins in front of you. Each time you reach in and scoop some out it is immediately refilled, no matter how many scoops you take. What is it like to experience being that supplied; To be that related to Source?

LAUGHTER!

☐ I laughed out loud for one minute today!

NOTES/LOG

_____
_____
_____
_____
_____
_____
_____
_____
_____

DAY THIRTEEN

"All that we are is the result of what we have thought. The mind is everything. What we think we become."

Buddha

EXPLORATION

Identify a belief or thought that limits you, or limits your experience of abundance. What is an example of that in your life? For example, "I don't have any marketable skills." Now create a new belief or thought in that area that inspires you. For example, "I am fulfilled in who I am now." Share it with your partner. (Tonight you will be using this new belief in your writing before bed.)

River Guide– Remember beliefs and thoughts can be handpicked.

BEING GRATEFUL

LISTEN TO SPIRIT

_____
_____
_____
_____
_____

BEING GENEROUS

Give some form of supply (money, food, clothes, time, etc.) to someone remembering money or supply doesn't go anywhere and releasing-receiving are ONE and the same.

Log Here

_____
_____

Did I acknowledge and thank _____ Me as the
            (Spirit word)   (Abundance word)

money, credit cards, plants, fishermen, shopkeepers, cooks, natural gas, truck drivers, etc. for participating in every meal and every product I used today?
Today I am especially acknowledging the postal service.

LISTENING AND SPEAKING AS SPIRIT

Partner A says:
My awareness, understanding and knowledge of the all providing activity of _____ expressing
(Spirit word)

within and as me is my supply. My awareness of this truth is unlimited so my supply is unlimited.

Partner B responds:
You _____ are _____
(Partner's name)   (Spirit word)

expressing as unlimited supply.

Repeat 11 times

Partner B says:
Your awareness, understanding and knowledge of the all providing activity of_____ expressing
(Spirit word)

within and as you is your supply. Your awareness of this truth is unlimited so your supply is unlimited.

Partner A responds:
I am _____ expressing as
(Spirit word)

unlimited supply.

Repeat 11 times

LAUGHTER!

☐ I laughed out loud for one minute today!

BEFORE BED

What I think, speak, believe, act and attitude is the source of my experience. Now write the new belief or thought you created earlier today 11 times.

NOTES/LOG

_____
_____
_____
_____
_____
_____
_____
_____
_____
_____
_____

DAY FIFTEEN

"If you judge people, you have no time to love them."

Mother Teresa

EXPLORATION

Whom do you have an opinion of that has you not really listen to them or be completely present with them? What's you're experience at those times?

River Guide– Can you see that opinions come from expectations, and expectations reduce the joy in life?

LAUGHTER!

☐ I laughed out loud for one minute today!

BEING GRATEFUL

Did I acknowledge and thank _____ Me as the
(Spirit word)   (Abundance word)

money, credit cards, plants, fishermen, shopkeepers, cooks, natural gas, truck drivers, etc. for participating in every meal and every product I used today?

Today I am especially acknowledging public transportation.

LISTEN TO SPIRIT

_____

_____

_____

_____

_____

BEING GENEROUS

Give away some form of supply (money, food, clothes, time, etc.) to someone, remembering money or supply doesn't go anywhere and releasing-receiving are ONE and the same.

Log Here

_____

_____

_____

_____

SPEAKING AND LISTENING AS SPIRIT

Partner A says:
I am adoring myself, I am adoring everyone else. I am the adoring love of
_____ radiating for myself and all.
(Spirit word)

Partner B responds:
You are _____'s love in expression.
(Spirit word)

Repeat 11 times

Partner B says:
You are adoring yourself, you are adoring everyone else. You are the adoring love of
_____ radiating for yourself and all.
(Spirit word)

Partner A responds:
I am _____'s love in expression.
(Spirit word)

Repeat 11 times

NOTES/LOG

_____
_____
_____
_____
_____
_____
_____
_____
_____

BEFORE BED

Sit quietly and start to write *I am the love of* _____ *in expression. I*
(Spirit word)
am the love of _____ *in action,*
(Spirit word)

I am enjoying being love now. As soon as you notice any thoughts you have that are contrary to that, write them down on a separate piece of paper and go back and start writing again. Do this exercise for 5 - 10 minutes...

Then tear up the piece of paper you wrote your contrary thoughts on and say out loud. "I am releasing - letting go of everything that is best for me to release now."

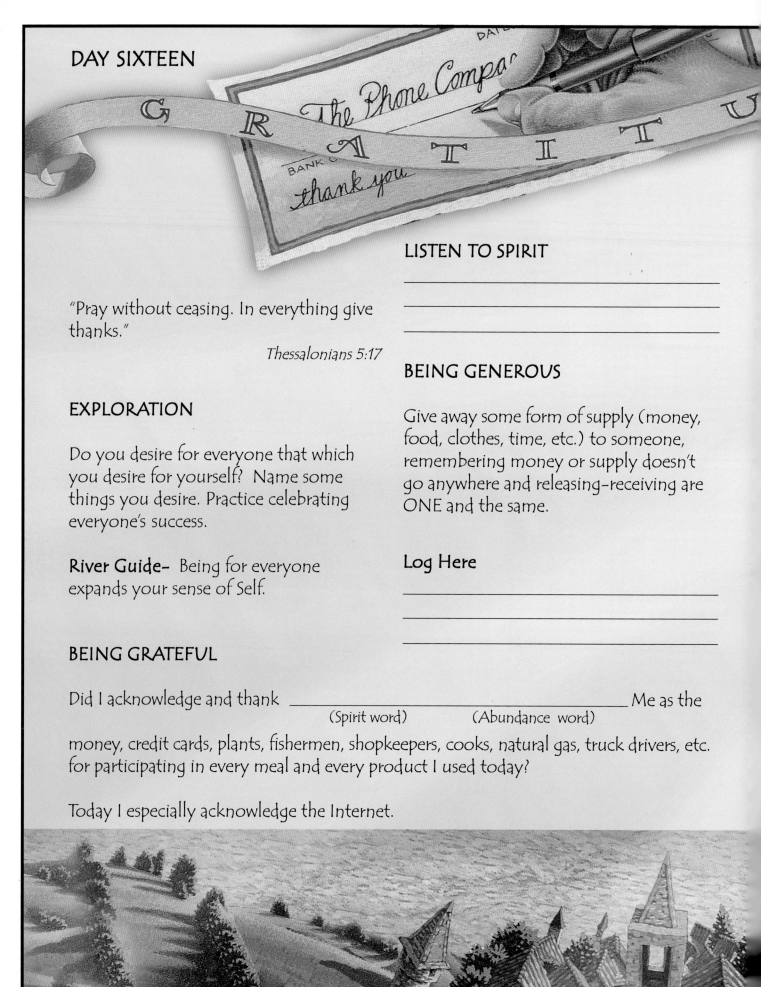

DAY SIXTEEN

"Pray without ceasing. In everything give thanks."

Thessalonians 5:17

EXPLORATION

Do you desire for everyone that which you desire for yourself? Name some things you desire. Practice celebrating everyone's success.

River Guide- Being for everyone expands your sense of Self.

BEING GRATEFUL

LISTEN TO SPIRIT

_____

_____

_____

BEING GENEROUS

Give away some form of supply (money, food, clothes, time, etc.) to someone, remembering money or supply doesn't go anywhere and releasing-receiving are ONE and the same.

Log Here

_____

_____

_____

Did I acknowledge and thank _____ Me as the
　　　　　　　　　　　　　　　(Spirit word)　　　(Abundance word)

money, credit cards, plants, fishermen, shopkeepers, cooks, natural gas, truck drivers, etc. for participating in every meal and every product I used today?

Today I especially acknowledge the Internet.

SPEAKING AND LISTENING AS SPIRIT

Partner A says:

_____ Me is being grateful
(Spirit word)

for all of life. I am grateful for

_____ now.
(choose something that is a stretch for you, ie:
phone company, Government, Mother-in-law)

Partner B responds:
You surrender to being grateful for all of
life now. You thank _____
(Spirit word)

as_____ in your life now.
(what you chose above)

Repeat 11 times

Partner B says:

_____ You is being grateful for
(Spirit word)

all of life. You are grateful for

_____ now.
(what you chose above)

Partner A responds:
I surrender to being grateful for
all of life now. I thank _____
as_____.(Spirit word)
(what you chose above)

Repeat 11 times

Now Partner A switch with Partner B so
that the focus of the exercise is reversed.

Repeat exercise

NOTES/LOG

_____
_____
_____
_____
_____
_____
_____
_____

LAUGHTER!

☐ I laughed out loud for one
minute today!

BEFORE BED

Say 11x to the person in
the mirror:
I am a cell in the body of the
Whole. I relish and love the
Whole of which I am part.

DAY SEVENTEEN

"Freely ye have received; freely give."
Matthew 10:8

EXPLORATION

Where do you hold back, resist giving or sharing completely?

River Guide- Releasing is an opportunity to be free, even God cannot fill what is already full.

LISTEN TO SPIRIT

_____
_____
_____
_____

BEING GENEROUS

Give away some form of supply (money, food, clothes, time, etc.) to someone, remembering money or supply doesn't go anywhere and releasing-receiving are ONE and the same.

Log Here

_____
_____
_____

BEING GRATEFUL

Did I acknowledge and thank _____ Me as the
(Spirit word)   (Abundance word)

money, credit cards, plants, fishermen, shopkeepers, cooks, natural gas, truck drivers, etc. for participating in every meal and every product I used today?

Today I am especially acknowledging soil.

SPEAKING AND LISTENING
AS SPIRIT

Partner A says:

I know giving and receiving are one and the same. I now give freely opening myself up to experiencing unlimited supply.

Partner B responds:

You now give freely experiencing
_____ GenerosityYou.
(Spirit word)

Repeat 11 times

Partner B says:

You know giving and receiving are one and the same. You now give freely opening yourself up to experiencing unlimited supply.

Partner A responds:

I now give freely experiencing
_____ Generosity Me.
(Spirit word)

Repeat 11 times

☐ LAUGHTER!

I laughed out loud for
one minute today!

BEFORE BED

Sit quietly, close your eyes and take a few deep breaths. Ask yourself what is something you are attached to or resist giving away? Why do you resist releasing it? Can you see that something might be available if you were willing to give it away?

(Remember it isn't about
giving it away, it is about
your willingness to let go.)

NOTES/LOG

_____
_____
_____
_____
_____
_____
_____
_____

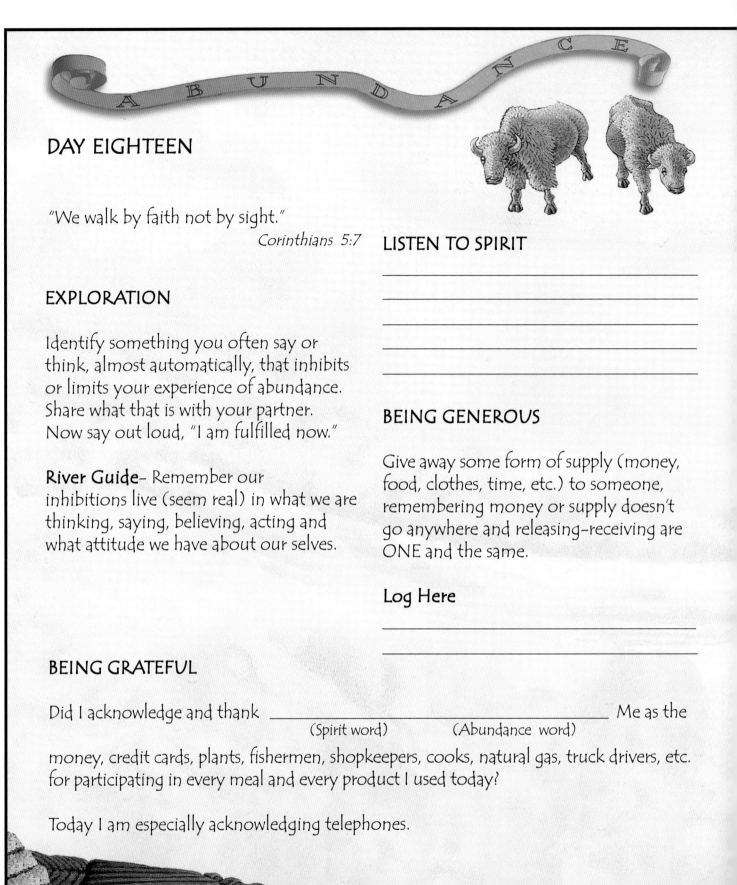

DAY EIGHTEEN

"We walk by faith not by sight."

Corinthians 5:7

EXPLORATION

Identify something you often say or think, almost automatically, that inhibits or limits your experience of abundance. Share what that is with your partner. Now say out loud, "I am fulfilled now."

River Guide- Remember our inhibitions live (seem real) in what we are thinking, saying, believing, acting and what attitude we have about our selves.

LISTEN TO SPIRIT

_____

_____

_____

_____

_____

BEING GENEROUS

Give away some form of supply (money, food, clothes, time, etc.) to someone, remembering money or supply doesn't go anywhere and releasing-receiving are ONE and the same.

Log Here

_____

_____

BEING GRATEFUL

Did I acknowledge and thank _____ Me as the
    (Spirit word)   (Abundance word)

money, credit cards, plants, fishermen, shopkeepers, cooks, natural gas, truck drivers, etc. for participating in every meal and every product I used today?

Today I am especially acknowledging telephones.

SPEAKING AND LISTENING AS SPIRIT

Partner A says:

I know the Divine _____ I am is
(Spirit word)

abundance so I am abundance. I love
perfect _____ Me completely. I
(Spirit word)

love all the abundance I see in form as
_____ Me now.
(Spirit word)   (Abundance word)

Partner B responds:

You know you are _____ and
(Spirit word)

_____ You is the only and
(Spirit word)

constant source of abundance.

Repeat 11 times

Partner B says:

You know the Divine _____ You are
(Spirit word)

is abundance so you are abundance. You
love perfect _____ You completely.
(Spirit word)

You love all the abundance you see in
form as _____
(Spirit word)   (Abundance word)

You now.

Partner A responds:

I know I am _____ and
(Spirit word)

_____ Me is the only and
(Spirit word)

constant source of abundance.

Repeat 11 times... Switch

BEFORE BED:

What is something you are resisting
buying for yourself because you don't
want to **spend** the money. Now list all
the people (manufacturer, retailer,
workers, banker, and all of their
families…) you would be contributing
to if you did purchase it for yourself.
Can you stand for being a contribution
to all those people?

LAUGHTER!

☐ I laughed out loud for
one minute today!

NOTES/LOG

_____
_____
_____
_____
_____
_____

DAY NINETEEN

"Without the assistance of the Divine Being I cannot succeed. With that assistance I cannot fail."

Abraham Lincoln

EXPLORATION

Say, I trust _____ Me as my
(Spirit word)

unlimited source and supply. Write down what your experience is when you say that.

River Guide- If you aren't trusting _____ who or what are you
(Spirit word)

trusting?

BEING GRATEFUL

Did I acknowledge and thank _____ Me as the
(Spirit word)   (Abundance word)

money, credit cards, plants, fishermen, shopkeepers, cooks, natural gas, truck drivers, etc. for participating in every meal and every product I used today?
Today I am especially acknowledging clothing.

LISTEN TO SPIRIT

_____

_____

_____

_____

_____

BEING GENEROUS

Give some form of supply (money, food, clothes, time, etc.) to someone remembering money or supply doesn't go anywhere and releasing-receiving are ONE and the same.

Log Here

_____

_____

LISTENING AND SPEAKING AS SPIRIT

Partner A says:
My life is a picture of my thoughts, speech, beliefs, actions and attitudes. I trust my experience of unlimited supply to keeping my attention on
_____ Me now.
(Spirit word)   (Abundance word)

Partner B responds:
You adore keeping your attention on
_____ You.
(Spirit word)   (Abundance word)

Repeat 11 times

Partner B says:
Your life is a picture of your thoughts, speech, beliefs, actions, and attitudes. You trust your experience of unlimited supply to keeping your attention on
_____ You now.
(Spirit word)   (Abundance word)

Partner A responds:
I adore keeping my attention on
_____ Me.
(Spirit word)   (Abundance word)

Repeat 11 times

Switch

LAUGHTER!

☐ I laughed out loud for one minute today!

BEFORE BED

(Write 11 times)
I choose _____ thoughts,
(Spirit word)
speech, beliefs, actions and attitudes all day long. I love choosing to live as
_____ Me.
(Spirit word)   (Abundance word)

NOTES/LOG

_____
_____
_____
_____
_____
_____
_____
_____
_____
_____
_____
_____

DAY TWENTY

"Your problem is you are too busy holding on to your unworthiness."

Ram Dass

EXPLORATION

Identify three ways of being (recurrents) you indulge in which diminish your experience of being worthy. For example, "I should be doing…", "I can't afford…", over eat…., etc. Now give yourself a hug and really appreciate how wonderful you are.

River Guide – Why not love yourself as you love others?

BEING GRATEFUL

LISTEN TO SPIRIT

_____
_____
_____
_____
_____

BEING GENEROUS

Give away some form of supply (money, food, clothes, time, etc.) to someone, remembering money or supply doesn't go anywhere and releasing-receiving are ONE and the same.

Log Here

_____
_____
_____

Did I acknowledge and thank _____ Me as the
(Spirit word)   (Abundance word)

money, credit cards, plants, fishermen, shopkeepers, cooks, natural gas, truck drivers, etc. for participating in every meal and every product I used today?

Today I am especially acknowledging mountains

LISTENING AND SPEAKING AS SPIRIT

Partner A says:

I know I am _____ . I am worthy of
(Spirit word)

all the abundance _____ Me is.
(Spirit word)

_____ is loving
(Spirit word)

having a _____ experience.
(Your name)

Partner B responds: You are loving
having a _____ experience. You
(Spirit word)

are all the abundance _____ You is.
(Spirit word)

Repeat 11 times

Partner B says:

You know you are _____ .
(Spirit word)

You are worthy of all the abundance

_____ You is. _____ is
(Spirit word)   (Spirit word)

loving having a _____ experience.
(Partner A's name)

Partner A responds:

I am loving having a _____
(Spirit word)

experience. I am all the abundance

_____ Me is.
(Spirit word)

Repeat 11 times... Switch

LAUGHTER!

☐ I laughed out loud for
one minute today!

BEFORE BED
(Say out loud 11 times in the mirror)
I now release any thoughts, speech,
beliefs, actions or attitudes of being
unworthy. I now honor and respect
myself as a _____ creation.
(Spirit word)

NOTES/LOG

_____
_____
_____
_____
_____
_____
_____
_____
_____

DAY TWENTY-ONE

"In the faces of men and women
I see God."

Walt Whitman

EXPLORATION
What do you notice or are aware of when you are really loving and accepting of yourself and others. What is that like for you? What is that like for the people in your community? Why not practice being loving and accepting always.

River Guide– There is only one of us.

LAUGHTER! ☐

I laughed out loud for one minute today!

BEING GRATEFUL

Did I acknowledge and thank _____ Me as the
(Spirit word)   (Abundance word)

money, credit cards, plants, fishermen, shopkeepers, cooks, natural gas, truck drivers, etc. for participating in every meal and every product I used today?

Today I especially acknowledge books.

LISTEN TO SPIRIT
_____
_____
_____
_____
_____

BEING GENEROUS

Give away some form of supply (money, food, clothes, time, etc.) to someone, remembering money or supply doesn't go anywhere and releasing-receiving are ONE and the same.

Log Here
_____
_____
_____
_____

NOTES/LOG

_____
_____
_____
_____
_____
_____
_____
_____

SPEAKING AND LISTENING AS SPIRIT

Partner A says:
I now choose to love and accept myself
and others as _____ . I celebrate
(Spirit word)

_____ Me in everyone I meet.
(Spirit word)

Partner B responds:
You celebrate _____ in you and in
(Spirit word)

everyone all day long.

Repeat 11 times

Partner B says:
You now choose to love and accept
yourself and others as _____ .
(Spirit word)

You celebrate _____ You in
(Spirit word)

everyone you meet.

Partner A responds:
I celebrate _____ in me and in
(Spirit word)

everyone all day long.

Repeat 11 times... Switch

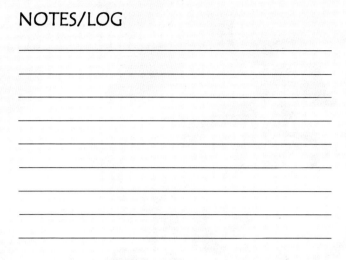

BEFORE BED
(Write 11 times)
I give up my judgments, assessments, and
opinions that the world should be some
other way. I love and accept others and
myself just the way we are. I trust
_____ 's creation.
(Spirit word)

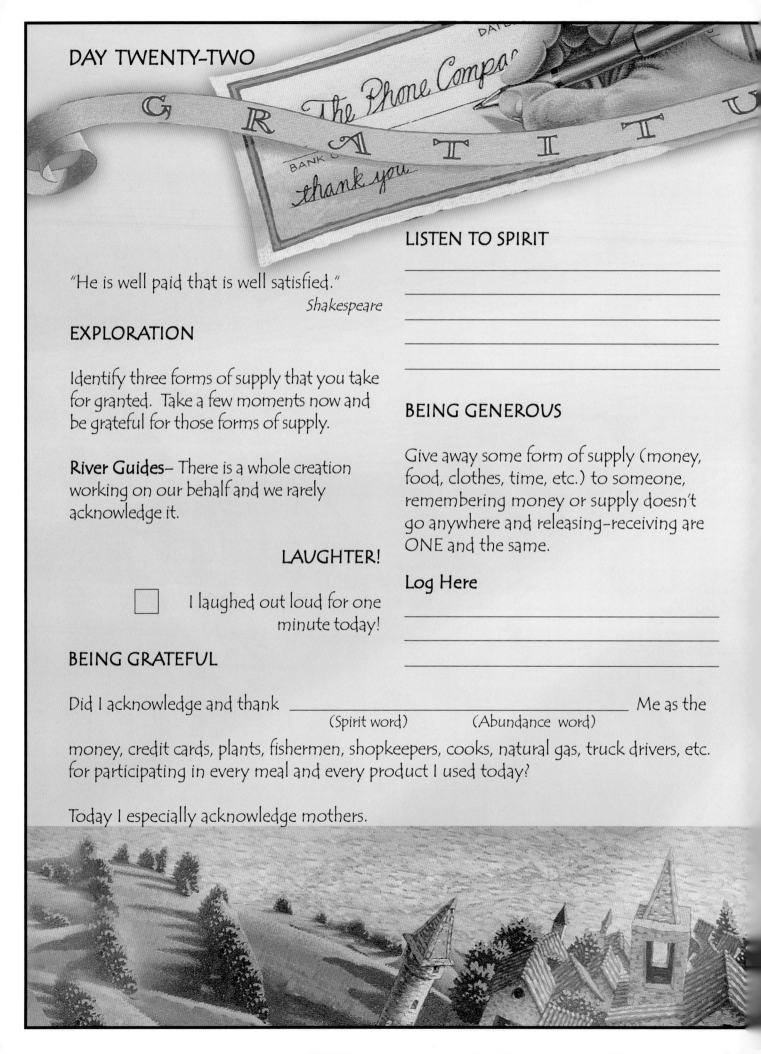

DAY TWENTY-TWO

"He is well paid that is well satisfied."
Shakespeare

EXPLORATION

Identify three forms of supply that you take for granted. Take a few moments now and be grateful for those forms of supply.

River Guides– There is a whole creation working on our behalf and we rarely acknowledge it.

LAUGHTER!

☐ I laughed out loud for one minute today!

BEING GRATEFUL

Did I acknowledge and thank _____ Me as the
(Spirit word)   (Abundance word)

money, credit cards, plants, fishermen, shopkeepers, cooks, natural gas, truck drivers, etc. for participating in every meal and every product I used today?

Today I especially acknowledge mothers.

LISTEN TO SPIRIT

_____
_____
_____
_____
_____

BEING GENEROUS

Give away some form of supply (money, food, clothes, time, etc.) to someone, remembering money or supply doesn't go anywhere and releasing-receiving are ONE and the same.

Log Here

_____
_____
_____

Partner A says: I am grateful for all the expressions of _____
(Spirit word + Abundance word)

Me. I acKnowledge and love money, food, shelter, vacations, hot showers, etc. as the out picturing of _____
(Spirit word)

_____ Me. I celebrate
(Abundance word)

_____ Me in form
(Spirit word + Abundance word)

and remember_____
(Spirit word + Abundance word)

Me as cause.

Partner B responds: You praise
_____ You in form
(Spirit word + Abundance word)

and as cause.

Repeat 11 times

NOTES/LOG

_____
_____
_____
_____
_____
_____
_____

Partner B says: You are grateful for all the expressions of _____
(Spirit word)

_____ You. You acknowledge
(Abundance word)

and love money, food, shelter, vacations, hot showers, etc. as the out picturing of _____ You. You
(Spirit word + Abundance word)

celebrate _____
(Spirit word + Abundance word)

You in form and remember

_____ You as cause.
(Spirit word + Abundance word)

Partner A responds:

I praise _____ Me
(Spirit word + Abundance word)

in form and as cause.

Repeat 11 times .... Switch

BEFORE BED
Write 11 times
I acknowledge the Divine in all forms of supply. I thank and am grateful to

_____ Me
(Spirit word + Abundance word)

for money, hot showers, vacations, credit cards, etc.

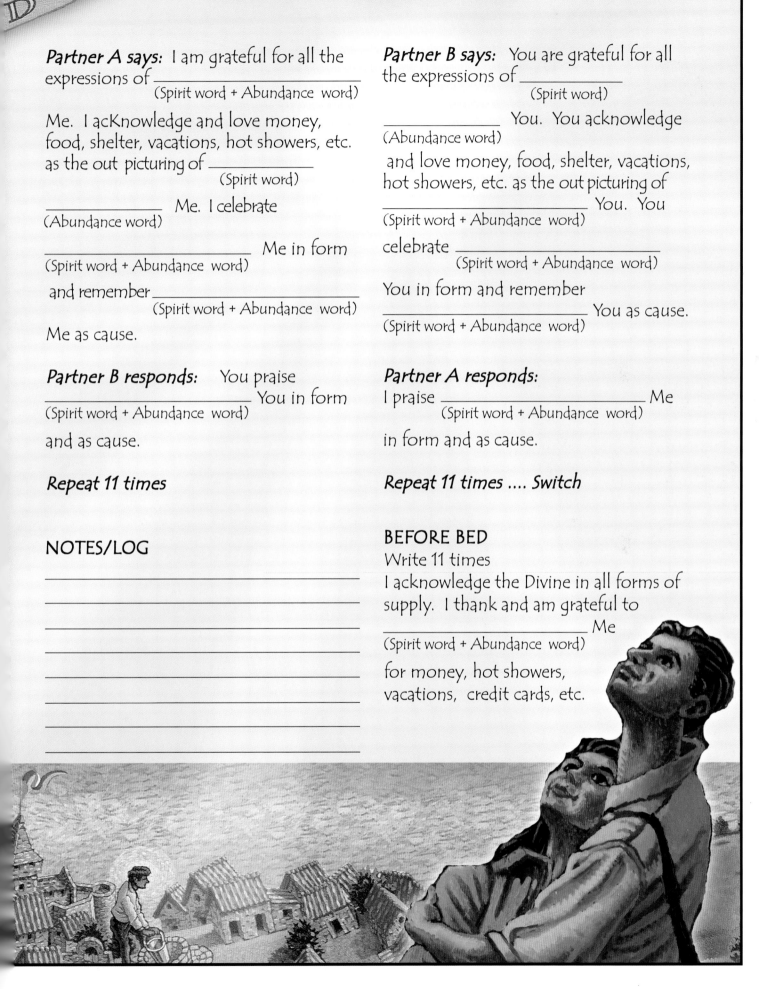

DAY TWENTY-THREE

"Nothing is enough to a man for whom enough is too little."

Epicures

EXPLORATION

What is your experience when you really give freely? Share with your partner. Give something away today you are attached to. Make a note of what you are going to give away

_____ .

River Guide– Where does it go anyway?

LISTEN TO SPIRIT

_____

_____

_____

_____

_____

BEING GENEROUS

Give away some form of supply (money, food, clothes, time, etc.) to someone, remembering money or supply doesn't go anywhere and releasing-receiving are ONE and the same.

Log Here

_____

_____

_____

BEING GRATEFUL

Did I acknowledge and thank _____ Me as the

(Spirit word)   (Abundance word)

money, credit cards, plants, fishermen, shopkeepers, cooks, natural gas, truck drivers, etc. for participating in every meal and every product I used today?

Today I especially acknowledge campfires.

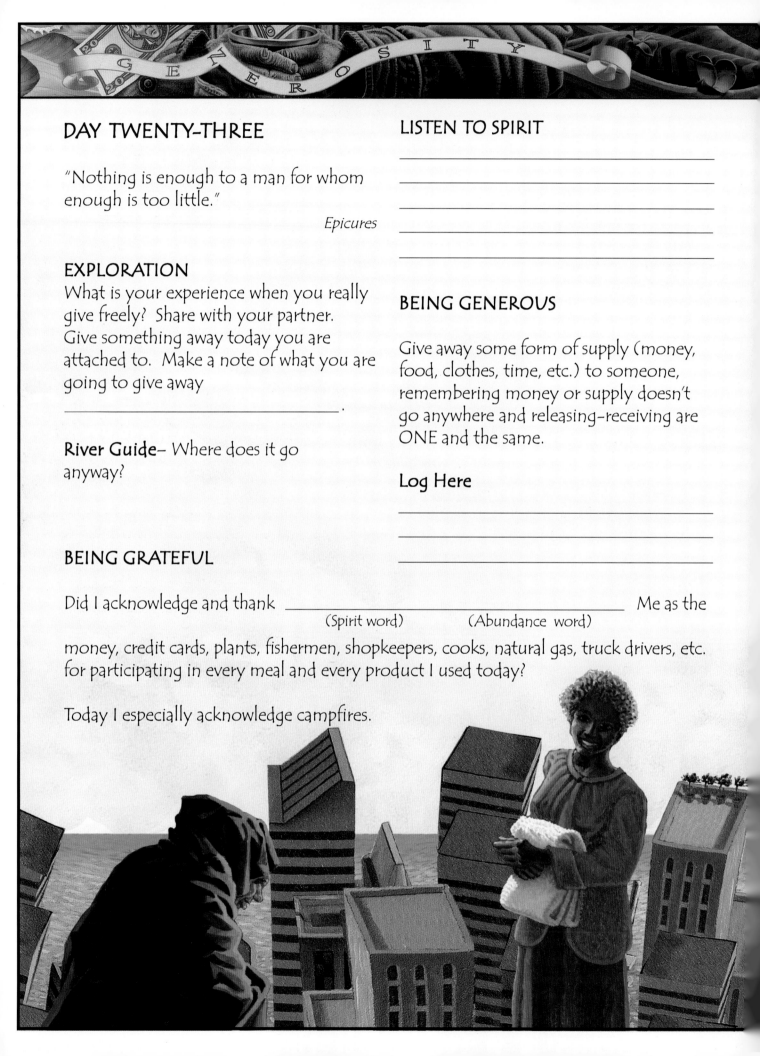

SPEAKING AND LISTENING AS SPIRIT

Partner A says:
I am a champion giver being _____,
Source and supply.   (Spirit word)

I am honored to share my blessed
abundance with everyone now.

Partner B responds:
You love _____ as everyone and
                (Spirit word)

are honored to share your blessed
abundance now.

Repeat 11 times

Partner B says: You are a champion giver
being _____ , Source and supply.
          (Spirit word)

You are honored to share your blessed
abundance with everyone now.

Partner A responds:
I love _____ as everyone and
            (Spirit word)

am honored to share my blessed
abundance now.

Repeat 11 times ... Switch

BEFORE BED
(write 11x)
I love giving freely to others with an
attitude of joy and service. I honor and
love _____ being_____
        (Spirit word)   (Spirit word)

Generosity Me.

☐ LAUGHTER!

I laughed out loud for
one minute today!

NOTES/LOG

_____
_____
_____
_____
_____
_____
_____
_____
_____

DAY TWENTY-FOUR

"There is a treasury of joy within you, why do you keep knocking door to door?"

Sufi saying

EXPLORATION

What is something you say you want that you can let go of wanting? Write that down on a sheet of paper and then tear it into pieces and throw it away. Say out loud, " I release wanting

_____ now."
(what you wrote down)

River Guide—Satisfaction isn't **out there** somewhere.

LISTEN TO SPIRIT

_____
_____
_____
_____
_____

BEING GENEROUS

Give away some form of supply (money, food, clothes, time, etc.) to someone, remembering money or supply doesn't go anywhere and releasing-receiving are ONE and the same.

Log Here

_____
_____
_____

BEING GRATEFUL

Did I acknowledge and thank _____ Me as the
(Spirit word)   (Abundance word)

money, credit cards, plants, fishermen, shopkeepers, cooks, natural gas, truck drivers, etc. for participating in every meal and every product I used today?

Today I especially acknowledge hot showers.

SPEAKING AND LISTENING AS SPIRIT

Partner A says:

I am enjoying letting go of wants I no longer need. I am completely fulfilled by the quality of abundance _____ Me

(Spirit word)

is being as me and as my life now.

Partner B responds:

You know _____ is being everything

(Spirit word)

you could ever desire. You are fulfilled by the quality of abundance _____

(Spirit word)
You is.

Repeat 11 times

Partner B says:

You are enjoying letting go of wants you no longer need. You are completely fulfilled by the quality of abundance _____ You is being as you and as

(Spirit word)

your life now.

Partner A responds:

I know _____ is being everything I

(Spirit word)

could ever desire. I am fulfilled by the quality of abundance _____ Me is.

(Spirit word)

Repeat 11 times

Switch

BEFORE BED:

(Write 11 times)

I am fulfilled being

_____ _____ Me now.

(Spirit word)   (Abundance word)

I let go and let _____ be my desire

(Spirit word)

and the fulfillment of my desires now.

LAUGHTER!

☐ I laughed out loud for one minute today!

NOTES/LOG

_____
_____
_____
_____
_____
_____
_____
_____

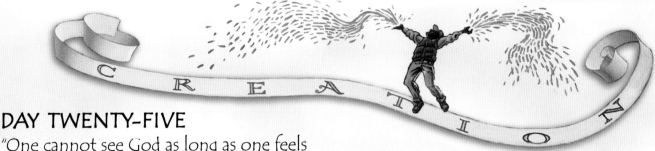

DAY TWENTY-FIVE

"One cannot see God as long as one feels I am the doer."

Rama Krishna

EXPLORATION

Identify a **recurrent** (reoccurring thought of limitation) you have around money. For example, "I never have enough" or "I can't make money doing what I love." Now what could you think practicing being satisfied and fulfilled now? Make a note of your created thought and share it with someone today.

River Guide- You can practice thinking anything. Why not practice thoughts that have you experience being part of one whole?

LISTEN TO SPIRIT

_____

_____

_____

_____

_____

BEING GENEROUS

Give away some form of supply (money, food, clothes, time, etc.) to someone, remembering money or supply doesn't go anywhere and releasing-receiving are ONE and the same.

Log Here

_____

_____

_____

BEING GRATEFUL

Did I acknowledge and thank _____ Me as the
(Spirit word)   (Abundance word)

money, credit cards, plants, fishermen, shopkeepers, cooks, natural gas, truck drivers, etc. for participating in every meal and every product I used today?
Today I am especially acknowledging the grass.

LAUGHTER!

☐ I laughed out loud for one minute today!

LISTENING AND SPEAKING AS SPIRIT

Partner A says:
I am one with all that is, everything I see and don't see. Everything I could ever desire I already am. I am whole and complete now.

Partner B responds:
What you want wants you. You are Spirit loving yourself, you are Spirit knowing itself.

Repeat 11 times

Partner B says:
You are one with all that is, everything you see and don't see. Everything you could ever desire you already are. You are whole and complete now.

Partner A responds:
What I want wants me. I am Spirit loving myself, I am Spirit knowing itself.

Repeat 11 times

Switch

BEFORE BED
Take the thought you created this morning and either write it 11 times or say it to yourself in the mirror, really embracing what you are saying.

NOTES/LOG

_____

_____

_____

_____

_____

_____

_____

DAY TWENTY-SIX

"Above all things, revere yourself."

Pythagoras

EXPLORATION

What would you love to be acknowledged or appreciated for? Today make a request of someone in your life to acknowledge or appreciate you for what you chose. Pick something that stretches your self worth.

River Guide– Why not love and appreciate yourself as

_____ 's perfect expression?

(Spirit word)

BEING GRATEFUL

Did I acknowledge and thank _____ Me as the

(Spirit word)   (Abundance word)

money, credit cards, plants, fishermen, shopkeepers, cooks, natural gas, truck drivers, etc. for participating in every meal and every product I used today?

Today I am especially acknowledging airplanes.

LISTEN TO SPIRIT

_____
_____
_____
_____
_____

BEING GENEROUS

Give away some form of supply (money, food, clothes, time, etc.) to someone, remembering money or supply doesn't go anywhere and releasing-receiving are ONE and the same.

Log Here

_____
_____
_____

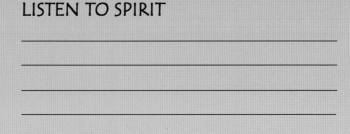

LISTENING AND SPEAKING AS SPIRIT

Partner A says:
I am perfect_____. I relish all of
(Spirit word)

myself. I love the whole_____
being I am.   _(Spirit word)_

Partner B responds:
I love myself as you; all of you. I
celebrate _____ as _____ and
          (Spirit word)   _(your name)_

_____.
(Your partner's name)

Repeat 11 times

Partner B says:
You are perfect _____ You
                (Spirit word)

relish all of yourself. You love the whole
_____ being you are.
(Spirit word)

Partner A responds:
You love your self as me; all of me. You
celebrate_____as_____
         (Spirit word) _(Your name)_
and _____ .
    (Your partner's name)

Repeat 11 times

... Switch

LAUGHTER!

☐ I laughed
out loud
for one
minute today!

BEFORE BED
(Say in the mirror 11 times)
I am Spirit's masterpiece. I admire
myself. I am Spirit revering it Self.

NOTES/LOG

_____
_____
_____
_____
_____
_____
_____
_____
_____

DAY TWENTY-SEVEN

L · O · V · E · · A · C · C · E · P · T · A · N · C · E

"When a dog runs at you, whistle for him."

Henry David Thoreau

EXPLORATION

Identify one relationship in your life where you are withholding love. How could you be more accepting so that LOVE would be present?
Today express love with that person.

River Guide– Look for someone with whom you don't experience love like you once did. Why would you let anything get in the way of Love?

LAUGHTER! ☐

I laughed out loud for one minute today!

BEING GRATEFUL

LISTEN TO SPIRIT

_____
_____
_____
_____
_____

BEING GENEROUS

Give away some form of supply (money, food, clothes, time, etc.) to someone, remembering money or supply doesn't go anywhere and releasing-receiving are ONE and the same.

Log Here

_____
_____
_____

Did I acknowledge and thank _____ Me as the
(Spirit word)   (Abundance word)

money, credit cards, plants, fishermen, shopkeepers, cooks, natural gas, truck drivers, etc. for participating in every meal and every product I used today?

Today I especially acknowledge butterflies.

SPEAKING AND LISTENING AS SPIRIT

Partner A says:

I love and accept others and myself as we are. I devote myself to _____ Me
(Spirit word)

by choosing to adore all of life in every now moment.

Partner B responds:

You devote your attention to being love and accepting all of life as whole perfect

_____.
(Spirit word)

Repeat 11 times

Partner B says:

You love and accept others and yourself as you are. You devote yourself to

_____ by choosing to adore all
(Spirit word)

of life in every now moment.

Partner A responds:

I devote my attention to being love and accepting all of life as whole perfect

_____.
(Spirit word)

Repeat 11 times

Switch

BEFORE BED

(Write 11 times)

_____ is being me and being
(Spirit word)

all the world now. _____ is
(Spirit word)

everywhere and is always present.   I am comfortable and peaceful knowing all is well and all is _____
(Spirit word)

NOTES/LOG

_____
_____
_____
_____
_____
_____
_____
_____

DAY TWENTY-EIGHT

LISTEN TO SPIRIT

_____
_____
_____
_____
_____

"If the only prayer you say in your whole life is Thank You, that would suffice."

Meister Eckhart

EXPLORATION

Express gratitude for some historical figure or event that has contributed to your life. For example, the fore Fathers of our country, our ancestors, leaders, wars, famines, the right to vote, etc.

River Guide– Can you see events we might or might not have agreed with have supported, even contributed to our lives?

☐ **LAUGHTER!**

I laughed out loud for one minute today!

BEING GRATEFUL

Did I acknowledge and thank _____ Me as the
         (Spirit word)   (Abundance word)

money, credit cards, plants, fishermen, shopkeepers, cooks, natural gas, truck drivers, etc. for participating in every meal and every product I used today?

Today I especially acknowledge oceans.

SPEAKING AND LISTENING AS SPIRIT

Partner A says:

I am grateful for all of life. I know
_____ is working in and through
  (Spirit word)

me for the best of all. I choose grateful
thoughts, grateful words, grateful actions,
grateful beliefs, and grateful actions all day
long.

Partner B responds:

You love being grateful. Being grateful you
are present to Perfect _____ You.
                              (Spirit word)

Repeat 11 times

Partner B says:

You are grateful for all of life. You know
_____ is working in and
  (Spirit word)

through you for the best of all. You choose
grateful thoughts, grateful words, grateful
beliefs, grateful actions and grateful
attitudes all day long.

Partner A responds:

I love being grateful. Being grateful I am
present to perfect _____ Me.
                         (Spirit word)

Repeat 11 times

Switch

NOTES/LOG

_____
_____
_____
_____
_____
_____
_____

BEING GENEROUS

Give away some form of supply (money,
food, clothes, time, etc.) to someone,
remembering money or supply doesn't
go anywhere and releasing-receiving are
ONE and the same.

Log Here

_____
_____
_____

BEFORE BED
Write 11 times
I choose being grateful.   Being
grateful brings to my awareness
Perfect _____ Me. I
              (Spirit word)

know_____is working
         (Spirit word)

in and through me now.

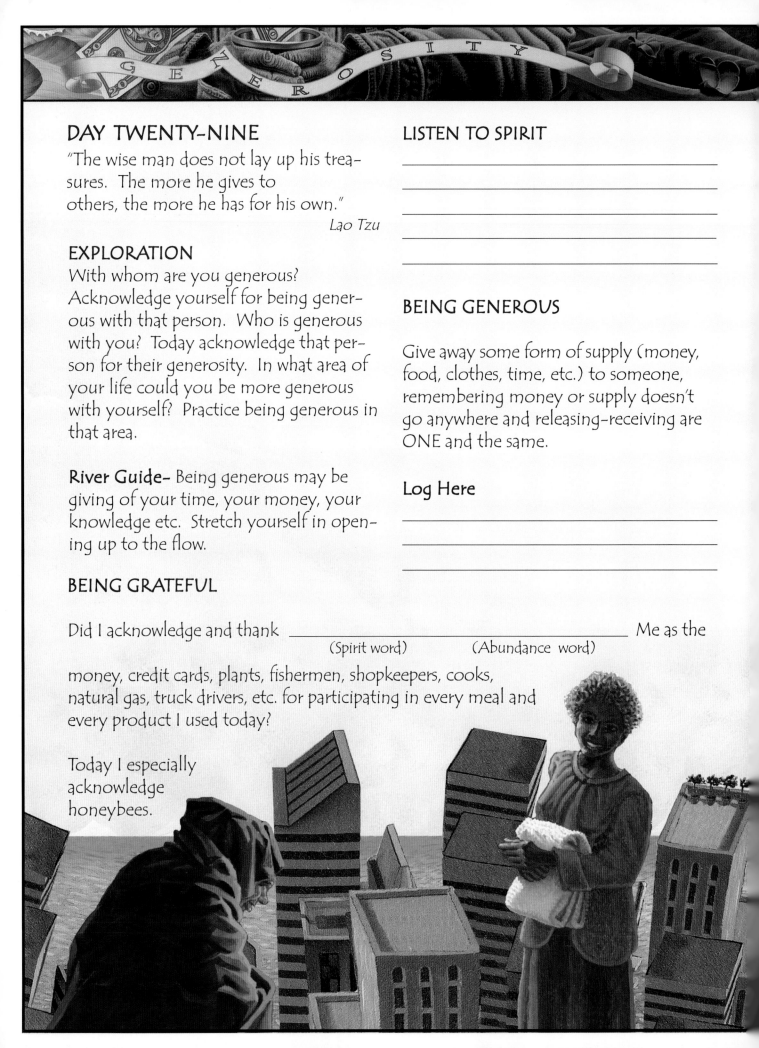

DAY TWENTY-NINE

"The wise man does not lay up his treasures. The more he gives to
others, the more he has for his own."

Lao Tzu

EXPLORATION

With whom are you generous?
Acknowledge yourself for being generous with that person. Who is generous
with you? Today acknowledge that person for their generosity. In what area of
your life could you be more generous
with yourself? Practice being generous in
that area.

River Guide- Being generous may be
giving of your time, your money, your
knowledge etc. Stretch yourself in opening up to the flow.

BEING GRATEFUL

Did I acknowledge and thank _____ Me as the
　　　　　　　　　　　　　　　　(Spirit word)　　　　(Abundance word)

money, credit cards, plants, fishermen, shopkeepers, cooks,
natural gas, truck drivers, etc. for participating in every meal and
every product I used today?

Today I especially
acknowledge
honeybees.

LISTEN TO SPIRIT

_____
_____
_____
_____
_____

BEING GENEROUS

Give away some form of supply (money,
food, clothes, time, etc.) to someone,
remembering money or supply doesn't
go anywhere and releasing-receiving are
ONE and the same.

Log Here

_____
_____
_____

SPEAKING AND LISTENING AS SPIRIT

Partner A says:

I know I am _____ . I know
(Spirit word)

I am Divine, I know I am whole and
complete so I choose to be Love and
give, give, give.

Partner B responds;

You are a divine giver, you practice being
_____ You by being generous.
(Spirit word)

Repeat 11 times

Partner B says:

You know you are _____ . You
(Spirit word)

know you are Divine. You know you are
whole and complete so you choose to be
Love and give, give, give.

Partner A responds:

I am a divine giver, I practice being
_____ Me by being generous.
(Spirit word)

Repeat 11 times

Switch

BEFORE BED

(write 11 times)
My Life is a picture of the generosity of
_____ and of _____
(Spirit word)   (Spirit word)

expressing as the generosity of others
in my life. I enjoy being generous
and contributing to others lives
as an expression of _____
(Spirit word)

_____ Me.
(Abundance word)

☐ LAUGHTER!

I laughed out loud for
one minute today!

NOTES/LOG

_____
_____
_____
_____
_____
_____
_____
_____
_____

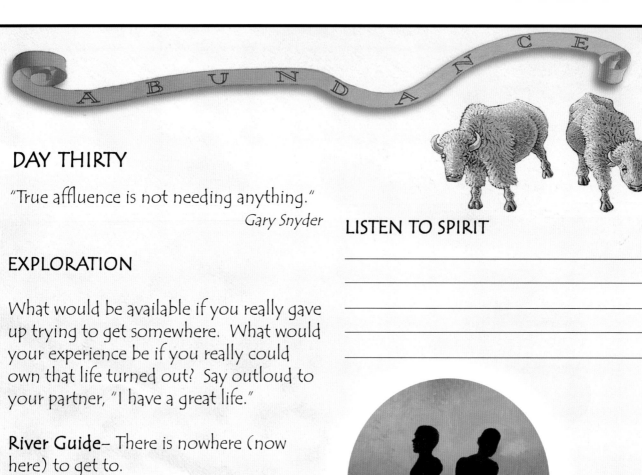

DAY THIRTY

"True affluence is not needing anything."
Gary Snyder

EXPLORATION

What would be available if you really gave up trying to get somewhere. What would your experience be if you really could own that life turned out? Say outloud to your partner, "I have a great life."

River Guide– There is nowhere (now here) to get to.

BEING GRATEFUL

Did I acknowledge and thank _____
(Spirit word)

_____ Me as the money,
(Abundance word)

credit cards, plants, fishermen, shop-keepers, cooks, natural gas, truck drivers, etc. for participating in every meal and every product I used today?

Today I am especially acknowledging musicians.

LISTEN TO SPIRIT

_____
_____
_____
_____

BEING GENEROUS

Give away some form of supply (money, food, clothes, time, etc.) to someone, remembering money or supply doesn't go anywhere and releasing-receiving are ONE and the same.

Log Here

_____
_____
_____

SPEAKING AND LISTENING AS SPIRIT

Partner A says:

My awareness of _____ as my
(Spirit word)

supply is my supply. I am present to
being lavishly fulfilled now.

Partner B responds:

You are aware of _____ as
(Spirit word)

_____ .You are all that is now.
(Abundance word)

Repeat 11 times

Partner B says:

Your awareness of _____ as your
(Spirit word)

supply is your supply. You are present to
being lavishly fulfilled now.

Partner A responds:

I am aware of _____ as
(Spirit word)

_____ .
(Abundance word)

I am all that is now.

Repeat 11 times... Switch

NOTES/LOG

_____
_____
_____
_____
_____
_____
_____
_____

LAUGHTER!

☐ I laughed out loud for
one minute today!

BEFORE BED:
(Write 11 times)
"I am fulfilled now. I am present to
being _____now."
(Abundance word)

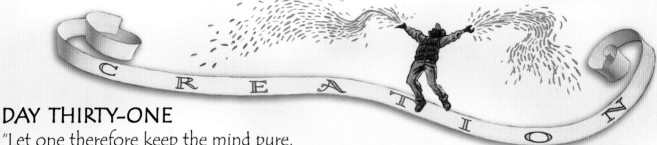

DAY THIRTY-ONE

"Let one therefore keep the mind pure,
for what a man thinks, that he becomes."

The Upanishads

EXPLORATION

Just for today practice thinking,
speaking, believing, acting and having an
attitude of, "I live a blessed life,"
all day. Bless everything, every
circumstance, and every person as an
opportunity to be _____ all day
                        (Spirit word)
long. Start your day by saying, "I live a
blessed life," out loud to yourself 7 times
in the mirror.

River Guide – You get to say how
your life is, why not create
it as blessed?"

BEING GRATEFUL

Did I acknowledge and thank _____ Me as the
                              (Spirit word)   (Abundance word)

money, credit cards, plants, fishermen, shopkeepers, cooks, natural gas, truck drivers, etc.
for participating in every meal and every product I used today?
Today I am especially grateful for fruit trees.

LISTEN TO SPIRIT

_____
_____
_____
_____
_____

BEING GENEROUS

Give away some form of supply (money,
food, clothes, time, etc.) to someone,
remembering money or supply doesn't
go anywhere and releasing-receiving are
ONE and the same.

Log Here

_____
_____
_____

LISTENING AND SPEAKING AS SPIRIT

Partner A says:

I adore _____ Me as my life now.
(Spirit word)

I honor _____ Me by keeping
(Spirit word)

my attention on the fullness of my life.
I am blessed now.

Partner B responds:

I thank you for your attention to
_____ You as the wholeness
(Spirit word)

you are. You are blessed now.

Repeat 11 times

Partner B says:

You adore _____ You as your
(Spirit word)

life now. You honor _____ You
(Spirit word)

by keeping your attention on the
fullness of your life. You are blessed now.

Partner A responds:

You thank me for my attention to
_____ Me as the wholeness I
(Spirit word)

am. I am blessed now.

Repeat 11 times

Switch

LAUGHTER!

☐ I laughed out loud for
one minute today!

BEFORE BED

Look back over your day and look for five
situations, experiences or people you
forgot to bless today. Be for them now.
Bless them as _____ You.
(Spirit word)

NOTES/LOG

_____
_____
_____
_____
_____
_____
_____

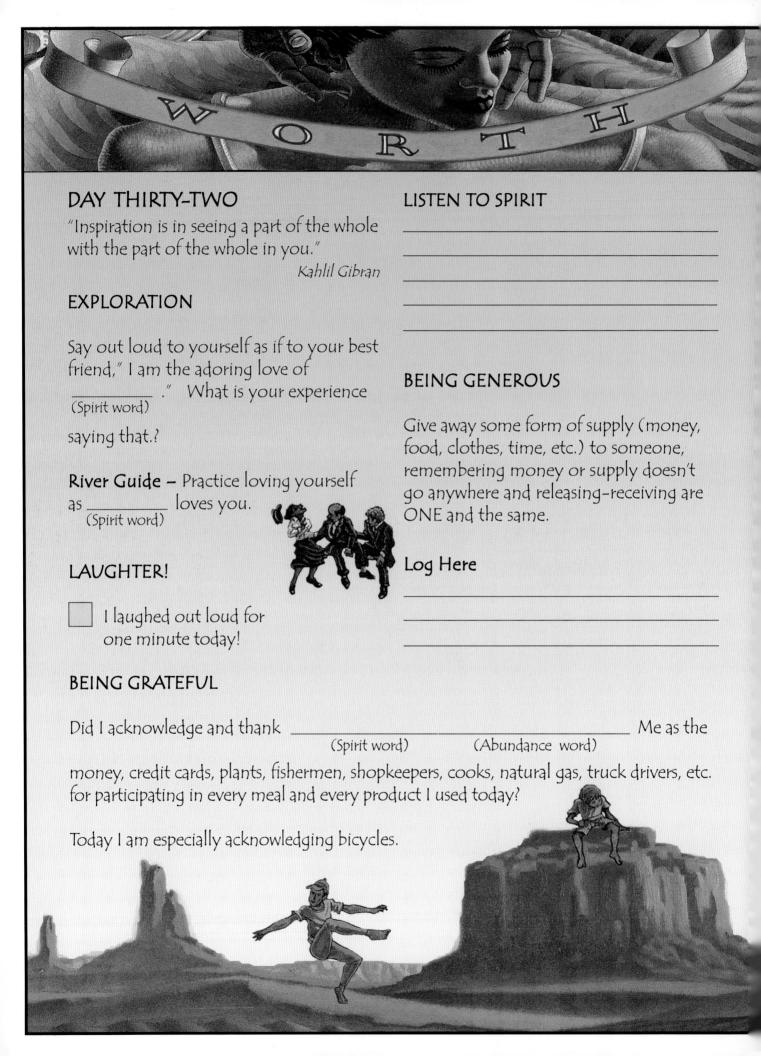

DAY THIRTY-TWO

"Inspiration is in seeing a part of the whole
with the part of the whole in you."

Kahlil Gibran

EXPLORATION

Say out loud to yourself as if to your best
friend," I am the adoring love of
_____ ."   What is your experience
(Spirit word)

saying that.?

River Guide – Practice loving yourself
as _____ loves you.
(Spirit word)

LAUGHTER!

☐ I laughed out loud for
one minute today!

BEING GRATEFUL

Did I acknowledge and thank _____ Me as the
(Spirit word)   (Abundance word)

money, credit cards, plants, fishermen, shopkeepers, cooks, natural gas, truck drivers, etc.
for participating in every meal and every product I used today?

Today I am especially acknowledging bicycles.

LISTEN TO SPIRIT

_____
_____
_____
_____
_____

BEING GENEROUS

Give away some form of supply (money,
food, clothes, time, etc.) to someone,
remembering money or supply doesn't
go anywhere and releasing-receiving are
ONE and the same.

Log Here

_____
_____
_____

LISTENING AND SPEAKING AS SPIRIT

Partner A says:

What I want wants me. I am everything
_____ is. I love and value myself
(Spirit word)

as a _____ creation.
(Spirit word)

Partner B responds:

You are a_____ masterpiece.
(Spirit word)

You adore yourself.

Repeat 11 times

Partner B says:

What you want wants you. You are
everything _____ is. You love and
(Spirit word)

value yourself as a _____ creation.
(Spirit word)

Partner A responds:

I am a _____ masterpiece. I adore
(Spirit word)

myself.

Repeat 11 times
...Switch

NOTES/LOG

_____
_____
_____
_____
_____
_____
_____
_____

BEFORE BED

Sit quietly for 10 minutes. Close your
eyes and take a few deep breaths. Thank
_____ You for revealing in what
(Spirit word)

area of your life you could be more
loving to yourself. Be grateful for what
you hear and log any appropriate actions
to take.

DAY THIRTY-THREE

"To love for the sake of being loved is human, but to love for the sake of loving is angelic."

Alphonse De LaMartine

EXPLORATION

Have a conversation with someone in your life listening to everything they say as "gold", Spirit's perfect expression. Grant them loving acceptance. Note your experience.

River Guide-

(Spirit word)

is everywhere and everyone.

LAUGHTER!

I laughed out loud for one minute today!

BEING GRATEFUL

Did I acknowledge and thank _____ Me as the
(Spirit word)   (Abundance word)

money, credit cards, plants, fishermen, shopkeepers, cooks, natural gas, truck drivers, etc. for participating in every meal and every product I used today?

Today I especially acknowledge sea life.

LISTEN TO SPIRIT

_____
_____
_____
_____
_____

BEING GENEROUS

Give away some form of supply (money, food, clothes, time, etc.) to someone, remembering money or supply doesn't go anywhere and releasing-receiving are ONE and the same.

Log Here

_____
_____
_____

SPEAKING AND LISTENING AS SPIRIT

Partner A says:
I love all of life as _____ Me.
(Spirit word)

Spirit Me is one and all the parts loving the Whole.

Partner B responds:
_____ You loves all of life,
(Spirit word)

all the expressions of the Whole.

Repeat 11 times

Partner B says:
You love all of life as _____ You.
(Spirit word)

Spirit You is one and all the parts loving the Whole.

Partner A responds:
_____ Me loves all of life,
(Spirit word)

all the expressions of the Whole.

Repeat 11 times... Switch

NOTES/LOG

_____

_____

_____

_____

_____

_____

BEFORE BED

Sit quietly. Close your eyes, take a few deep breaths. See yourself as a cell in the body of the whole of life, one body working in perfect harmony. Every cell in this body is doing it's perfect work and receiving exactly what it requires. Now put your attention on a part (a person, event, condition) of the Whole, some part you don't accept as perfect. Next thank _____ for revealing to you
(Spirit word)

the opportunity this part of the Whole is.

Be grateful for this guidance and log any appropriate action to take.

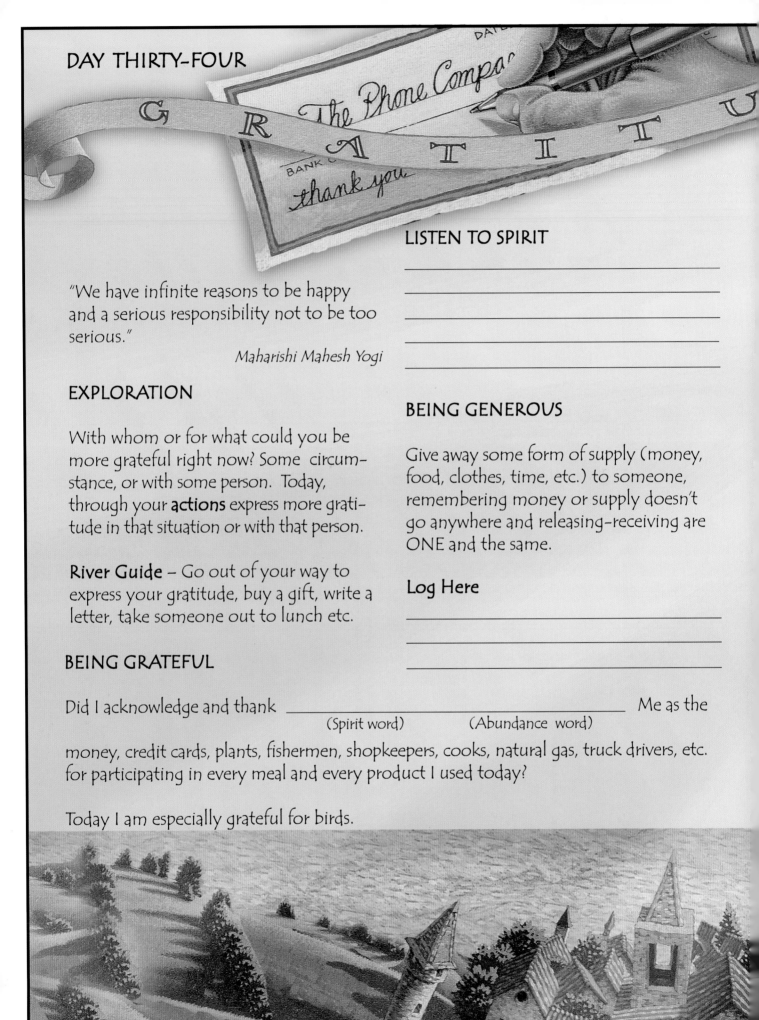

DAY THIRTY-FOUR

"We have infinite reasons to be happy and a serious responsibility not to be too serious."

Maharishi Mahesh Yogi

EXPLORATION

With whom or for what could you be more grateful right now? Some circumstance, or with some person. Today, through your **actions** express more gratitude in that situation or with that person.

River Guide – Go out of your way to express your gratitude, buy a gift, write a letter, take someone out to lunch etc.

BEING GRATEFUL

Did I acknowledge and thank _____ Me as the
(Spirit word)   (Abundance word)

money, credit cards, plants, fishermen, shopkeepers, cooks, natural gas, truck drivers, etc. for participating in every meal and every product I used today?

Today I am especially grateful for birds.

LISTEN TO SPIRIT

_____
_____
_____
_____
_____

BEING GENEROUS

Give away some form of supply (money, food, clothes, time, etc.) to someone, remembering money or supply doesn't go anywhere and releasing-receiving are ONE and the same.

Log Here

_____
_____
_____

SPEAKING AND LISTENING AS SPIRIT

Partner A says:

I am grateful for all that is, every expression of _____ . Grateful is
(Spirit word)

who I am and who _____ is. I
(Spirit word)

bring being grateful to every moment.

Partner B responds:

You are _____ being grateful now.
(Spirit word)

Repeat 11 times

Partner B says:

You are grateful for all that is, every expression of _____. Grateful is
(Spirit word)

who you are and who _____ is. You
(Spirit word)

bring being grateful to every moment.

Partner A responds:

I am _____ being grateful now.
(Spirit word)

Repeat 11 times

Switch

NOTES/LOG

_____

_____

_____

_____

_____

_____

_____

LAUGHTER!

I laughed out loud for one minute today!

BEFORE BED

Write 11x before going to bed.

I am an instrument of gratitude. I bless
_____ Me as all of life all day long.
(Spirit word)

DAY THIRTY-FIVE

"Kindness costs nothing."

Irish Proverb

EXPLORATION

Consider all the things, possessions, you have take up space, physical, mental, emotional, and spiritual. Consider that everything you aren't relishing is occupying the space for something new. Release something today making room for the new.

River Guide– If you aren't relishing something release it.

BEING GRATEFUL

Did I acknowledge and thank _____ Me as the
(Spirit word)   (Abundance word)

money, credit cards, plants, fishermen, shopkeepers, cooks, natural gas, truck drivers, etc. for participating in every meal and every product I used today?

Today I am especially acknowledging the earth.

LISTEN TO SPIRIT

_____

_____

_____

_____

_____

BEING GENEROUS

Give away some form of supply (money, food, clothes, time, etc.) to someone, remembering money or supply doesn't go anywhere and releasing-receiving are ONE and the same.

Log Here

_____

_____

_____

SPEAKING AND LISTENING AS SPIRIT

Partner A says:

As I give, I bless the Whole of myself. As I receive, I honor all that _____
(Spirit word)
Me is.

Partner B responds:

Your releasing and receiving celebrates Whole_____ You.
(Spirit word)

Repeat 11 times

Partner B says:

As you give, you bless the Whole of your self. As you receive, you honor all that _____ You is.
(Spirit word)

Partner A responds:

My releasing and receiving celebrates Whole_____ Me.
(Spirit word)

Repeat 11 times

Switch

BEFORE BED
(write 11 times)

I relish releasing and receiving as being part of the whole of life. I love being in the flow of_____ 's supply.
(Spirit word)

☐ LAUGHTER!

I laughed out loud for one minute today!

NOTES

_____
_____
_____
_____
_____
_____
_____
_____

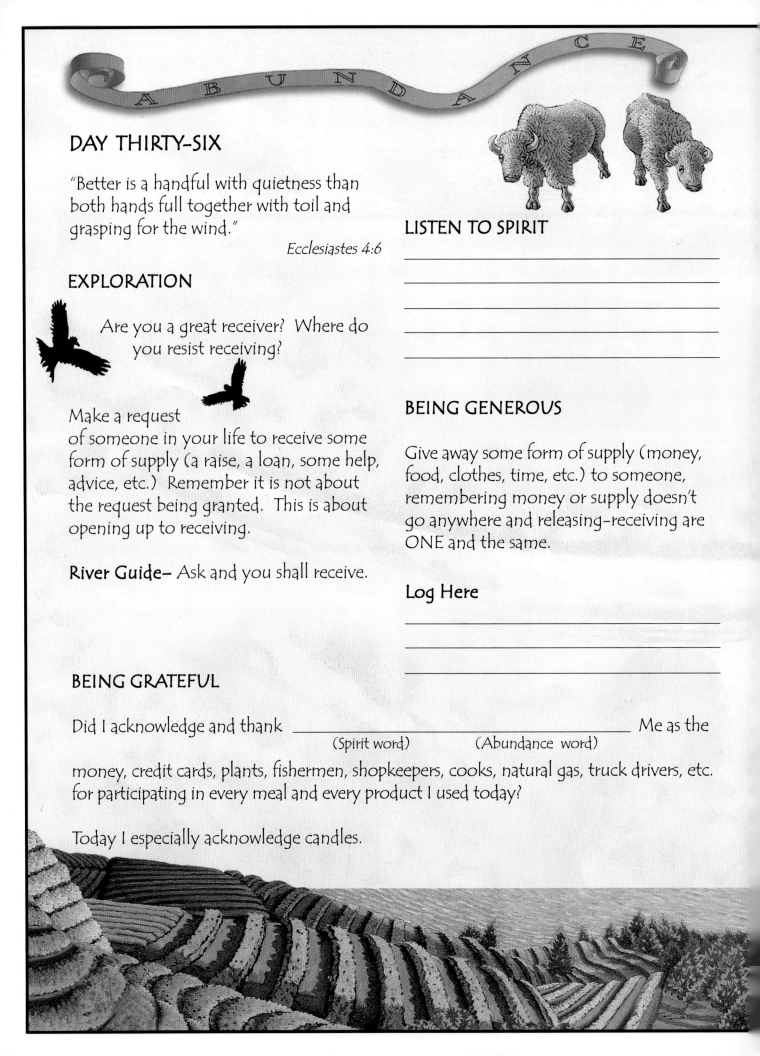

ABUNDANCE

DAY THIRTY-SIX

"Better is a handful with quietness than both hands full together with toil and grasping for the wind."

Ecclesiastes 4:6

EXPLORATION

Are you a great receiver? Where do you resist receiving?

Make a request of someone in your life to receive some form of supply (a raise, a loan, some help, advice, etc.) Remember it is not about the request being granted. This is about opening up to receiving.

River Guide– Ask and you shall receive.

LISTEN TO SPIRIT

_____
_____
_____
_____
_____

BEING GENEROUS

Give away some form of supply (money, food, clothes, time, etc.) to someone, remembering money or supply doesn't go anywhere and releasing-receiving are ONE and the same.

Log Here

_____
_____
_____

BEING GRATEFUL

Did I acknowledge and thank _____ Me as the
(Spirit word)   (Abundance word)

money, credit cards, plants, fishermen, shopkeepers, cooks, natural gas, truck drivers, etc. for participating in every meal and every product I used today?

Today I especially acknowledge candles.

SPEAKING AND LISTENING AS SPIRIT

Partner A says:

I am_____ so I am Wholeness
    (Spirit word)
now. I relish keeping my attention on being fulfilled.

Partner B responds:

You are _____ present to your
    (Spirit word)
Wholeness now.

Repeat 11 times

Partner B says:

You are _____ so you are
    (Spirit word)
Wholeness now. You relish keeping your attention on being fulfilled.

Partner A responds:

I am_____ present to my
    (Spirit word)
Wholeness now.

Repeat 11 times

Switch

NOTES/LOG

_____
_____
_____
_____
_____
_____
_____
_____

LAUGHTER!

☐ I laughed out loud for one minute today!

BEFORE BED

(Write 11 times)
"I give up getting somewhere. I am present to being fulfilled now."

DAY THIRTY-SEVEN

"Perception is a learned phenomenon."

Deepak Chopra

EXPLORATION

1. Introduce yourself to 3 people today as your_____ name.
   (Spirit word) (Abundance word)

2. Put your _____
   (Spirit word) (Abundance word)

name on your voicemail.

3. What's your experience with these requests? If you experience resistance, notice what names that which is resisting (ego) calls you. For example; lazy, fat, unorganized, etc.

River Guide– If you can't call yourself _____ , what are
(Spirit word) (Abundance word)

you committed to?

BEING GRATEFUL

Did I acknowledge and thank _____ Me as the
(Spirit word)   (Abundance word)

money, credit cards, plants, fishermen, shopkeepers, cooks, natural gas, truck drivers, etc. for participating in every meal and every product I used today?
Today I especially acknowledge insects.

LISTEN TO SPIRIT

_____
_____
_____
_____
_____

BEING GENEROUS

Give away some form of supply (money, food, clothes, time, etc.) to someone, remembering money or supply doesn't go anywhere and releasing-receiving are ONE and the same.

Log Here

_____
_____
_____

LISTENING AND SPEAKING AS SPIRIT

Partner A says:
Who I am being (thinking, speaking, believing, acting and ttituding) creates my experience of life. Whatever experience I am having, I am creating that. I now choose to love my life.

Partner B responds:
Knowing you create your experience of life, you choose to love your life now.

Repeat 11 times

Partner B says:
Who you are being (thinking, speaking, believing, acting and attituding) creates your experience of life. Whatever experience you are having you are creating that. You now choose to love your life.

Partner A responds:
Knowing I create my experience of life, I choose to love my life now.

Repeat 11 times... Switch

LAUGHTER!

I laughed out loud for one minute today!

BEFORE BED

Go through your day. Notice where you were not being completely responsible, where you were living like there was a world **out there,** happening to you. Now recreate that same situation as an opportunity to awaken to _____ You.

(Spirit word)

Now write 11 times
I am_____ awakening to myself.

(Spirit word)

NOTES/LOG

_____

_____

_____

_____

_____

_____

_____

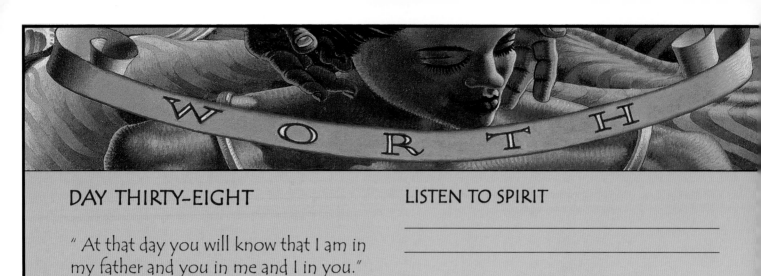

DAY THIRTY-EIGHT

" At that day you will know that I am in
my father and you in me and I in you."

John 14:20

EXPLORATION

If you could choose to be known for any
quality of character or any way of being,
what would you love to be known for?
For example, thoughtful, generous, kind,
loving, courageous, etc. Look yourself in
the mirror and acknowledge yourself for
being that way.

River Guide-
What are you waiting for?

BEING GRATEFUL

LISTEN TO SPIRIT

_____
_____
_____
_____
_____

BEING GENEROUS

Give away some form of supply (money,
food, clothes, time, etc.) to someone,
remembering money or supply doesn't
go anywhere and releasing-receiving are
ONE and the same.

Log Here

_____
_____
_____

Did I acknowledge and thank _____ Me as the
　　　　　　　　　　　　　　　(Spirit word)　　　　　(Abundance word)

money, credit cards, plants, fishermen, shopkeepers, cooks, natural gas, truck drivers, etc.
for participating in every meal and every product I used today?

Today I am especially acknowledging hummingbirds.

LISTENING AND SPEAKING AS SPIRIT

Partner A says:

I am a Divine creation. I honor
_____ by adoring myself.
(Spirit word)

Partner B responds:

You are worthy of everything
_____ is. You love
(Spirit word)

_____ as you.
(Spirit word)

Repeat 11 times

Partner B says:

You are a Divine creation. You honor
_____ by adoring yourself.
(Spirit word)

Partner A responds:

I am worthy of everything _____ is.
(Spirit word)

I love _____ as me.
(Spirit word)

Repeat 11 times

Switch

LAUGHTER!

☐ I laughed out loud for
one minute today!

BEFORE BED

(11x in the mirror with body movements)
I am adoring myself. I am adoring everyone else. I am the adoring love of
_____ radiating for myself
(Spirit word)

and all.

NOTES/LOG

_____
_____
_____
_____
_____
_____
_____
_____

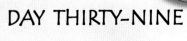

DAY THIRTY-NINE

"We are not held back by the love we didn't receive in the past, but by the love we're not extending in the present."
Marianne Williamson

EXPLORATION

What do you resist or not accept about your finances? Now share with your partner what you could say about that same situation that would have you experience acceptance.

River Guide– What you resist will persist, Loving and accepting gets you out of your own way.

LAUGHTER!

I laughed out loud for one minute today!

BEING GRATEFUL

Did I acknowledge and thank _____ Me as the
(Spirit word)   (Abundance word)

money, credit cards, plants, fishermen, shopkeepers, cooks, natural gas, truck drivers, etc. for participating in every meal and every product I used today?

Today I am especially acknowledging fathers.

LISTEN TO SPIRIT

_____
_____
_____
_____
_____

BEING GENEROUS

Give away some form of supply (money, food, clothes, time, etc.) to someone, remembering money or supply doesn't go anywhere and releasing-receiving are ONE and the same.

Log Here

_____
_____
_____

SPEAKING AND LISTENING AS SPIRIT

Partner A says:

_____ is being my life and being
(Spirit word)

all of life. I trust _____ and bless
(Spirit word)

_____ in and as everything.
(Spirit word)

Partner B responds:

_____ loves being you and being
(Spirit word)

all of life. You love being_____ .
(Spirit word)

Repeat 11 times

Partner B says:

_____ is being your life and
(Spirit word)

being all of life. You trust_____
(Spirit word)

and bless_____ in and as
(Spirit word)

everything.

Partner A responds:

_____ loves being me and being
(Spirit word)

all of life. I love being_____ .
(Spirit word)

Repeat 11 times

Switch

BEFORE BED

Sit quietly and go over your day in your mind. Did you presence love everywhere and with everyone? (For example; at the bank, the grocery store, with people at work) Did you give everyone an opportunity to experience their greatness? Did you greet everyone as a child of God, your brother or sister? Now go back through your day and imagine extending more love in those same encounters.

NOTES/LOG

_____

_____

_____

_____

_____

_____

_____

_____

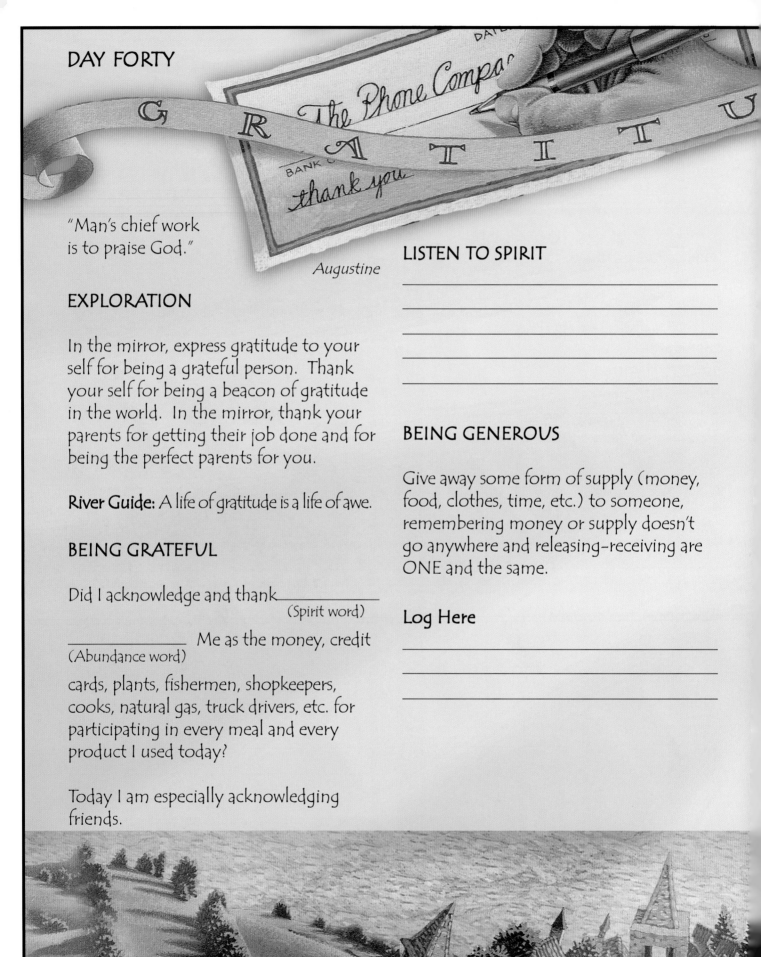

DAY FORTY

"Man's chief work is to praise God."

Augustine

EXPLORATION

In the mirror, express gratitude to your self for being a grateful person. Thank your self for being a beacon of gratitude in the world. In the mirror, thank your parents for getting their job done and for being the perfect parents for you.

River Guide: A life of gratitude is a life of awe.

BEING GRATEFUL

Did I acknowledge and thank_____
(Spirit word)

_____ Me as the money, credit
(Abundance word)

cards, plants, fishermen, shopkeepers, cooks, natural gas, truck drivers, etc. for participating in every meal and every product I used today?

Today I am especially acknowledging friends.

LISTEN TO SPIRIT

_____
_____
_____
_____
_____

BEING GENEROUS

Give away some form of supply (money, food, clothes, time, etc.) to someone, remembering money or supply doesn't go anywhere and releasing-receiving are ONE and the same.

Log Here

_____
_____
_____

SPEAKING AND LISTENING AS SPIRIT

Partner A says:

I greet everything _____ Me is
                    (Spirit word)

with gratitude. Being grateful is my living prayer.

Partner B responds:

You relish and bless all that
_____ Me is. You embody
(Spirit word)

gratitude.

Repeat 11 times

Partner B says:

You greet everything _____ You
                    (Spirit word)

is with gratitude. Being grateful is your living prayer.

Partner A responds:

I relish and bless all that
_____ You is.
(Spirit word)

Repeat 11 times

Switch

NOTES

_____
_____
_____
_____
_____
_____
_____

LAUGHTER!

☐ I laughed out loud for one minute today!

BEFORE BED

Call someone tonight and thank him or her for loving you, for being in your life. Express your gratitude to them.

GENEROSITY

DAY FORTY-ONE

"We are not isolated islands, we are joined to one another like the links in a chain."

Ammachi

EXPLORATION

Are you as generous as you'd love to be? If not, what stops you from being more generous? What act of generosity could you take on today that would be a stretch for you? Follow through with that action

River Guide- Generosity breaks down all barriers of separation.

BEING GRATEFUL

Did I acknowledge and thank _____ Me as the money, credit
(Spirit word)　　　　(Abundance word)

cards, plants, fishermen, shopkeepers, cooks, natural gas, truck drivers, etc. for participating in every meal and every product I used today?

Today I am especially acknowledging friends.

LISTEN TO SPIRIT

_____
_____
_____
_____
_____

BEING GENEROUS

Give away some form of supply (money, food, clothes, time, etc.) to someone, remembering money or supply doesn't go anywhere and releasing-receiving are ONE and the same.

Log Here

_____
_____
_____

SPEAKING AND LISTENING AS SPIRIT

Partner A says:
In giving I presence wholeness for myself and all. I am _____ Me sharing
(Spirit word)

with _____ Wholeness.
(Spirit word)

Partner B responds:
You are _____ being present to
(Spirit word)

_____ . You are the presence of
(Spirit word)

Wholeness.

Repeat 11 times

Partner B says:
In giving you presence wholeness for yourself and all. You are _____
(Spirit word)

You sharing with _____
(Spirit word)
Wholeness.

Partner A responds:
I am _____ Me being present to
(Spirit word)

_____ . I am the presence of
(Spirit word)
Wholeness.

Repeat 11 times   ...Switch

BEFORE BED

Sit quietly and close your eyes. Keep your awareness on your breath. Notice your inhale (receive) and exhale (release). Be present to all the supply you receive on the inhale and all that you release on the exhale. Be grateful for the constant flow of supply that moves through you. Be present to releasing and receiving.

☐ LAUGHTER!

I laughed out loud for one minute today!

NOTES/LOG

_____
_____
_____
_____
_____
_____

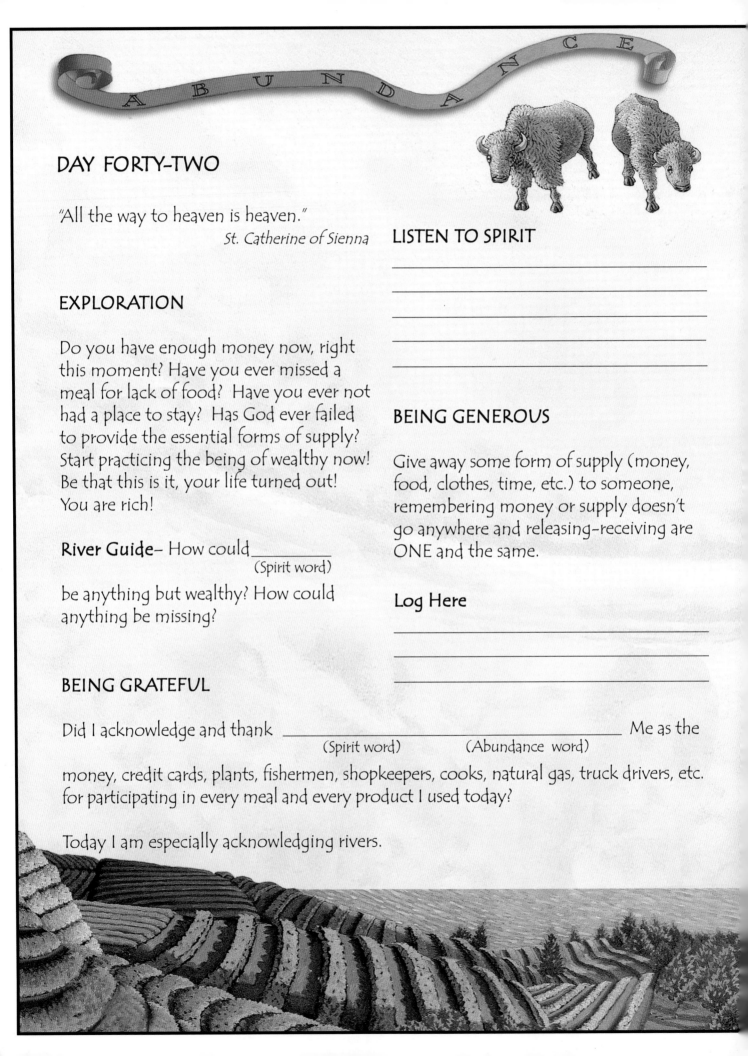

ABUNDANCE

DAY FORTY-TWO

"All the way to heaven is heaven."
St. Catherine of Sienna

EXPLORATION

Do you have enough money now, right this moment? Have you ever missed a meal for lack of food? Have you ever not had a place to stay? Has God ever failed to provide the essential forms of supply? Start practicing the being of wealthy now! Be that this is it, your life turned out! You are rich!

River Guide– How could _____
(Spirit word)

be anything but wealthy? How could anything be missing?

BEING GRATEFUL

Did I acknowledge and thank _____ Me as the
(Spirit word)   (Abundance word)

money, credit cards, plants, fishermen, shopkeepers, cooks, natural gas, truck drivers, etc. for participating in every meal and every product I used today?

Today I am especially acknowledging rivers.

LISTEN TO SPIRIT

_____

_____

_____

_____

_____

BEING GENEROUS

Give away some form of supply (money, food, clothes, time, etc.) to someone, remembering money or supply doesn't go anywhere and releasing-receiving are ONE and the same.

Log Here

_____

_____

_____

SPEAKING AND LISTENING AS SPIRIT

Partner A says:
I honor _____ and relish all
        (Spirit word)

that _____ has given. I am
    (Spirit word)

abundance now.

Partner B responds:
In and through you _____
           (Spirit word)

expresses as abundance. You give your
life to being abundance now.

Repeat 11 times

Partner B says:
You honor _____ and relish all
        (Spirit word)

that _____ has given. You are
    (Spirit word)

abundance now.

Partner A responds:
In and through me _____ expresses
         (Spirit word)

as abundance. I give my life
to being abundance now.

Repeat 11 times

Switch

BEFORE BED

(Write 11 times)
"I am releasing my habit of *something's missing*. I am that I am abundance now."

☐ LAUGHTER!

I laughed out loud for one minute today!

NOTES/LOG

_____
_____
_____
_____
_____
_____
_____
_____